Tony Kubalak

CARVING 18th-CENTURY AMERICAN FURNITURE MOTIFS

4880 Lower Valley Road · Atglen, PA 19310

Other Schiffer Books on Related Subjects:

Making Classic Carved Furniture: The Queen Anne Stool, Ron Clarkson & Tom Heller, ISBN 978-0-88740-588-4

Classic Carved Furniture: Making a Piecrust Tea Table, Tom Heller & Ron Clarkson, ISBN 978-0-88740-616-4

Library of Congress Control Number: 2016958537

Designed by Brenda McCallum
Cover design by Justin Watkinson
Cover photo by Ramon Moreno
Type set in Engraves MT / Helvetica

ISBN: 978-0-7643-5236-2
Printed in China

Published by Schiffer Publishing, Ltd.
4880 Lower Valley Road
Atglen, PA 19310
Phone: (610) 593-1777; Fax: (610) 593-2002
E-mail: Info@schifferbooks.com
Web: www.schifferbooks.com

In memory of Gene Landon who inspired and motivated me to achieve things I did not think possible.

DEDICATION

To my wife Barb and our son Peter; if not for you everything would mean so much less.

CONTENTS

Swan Neck Molding
7–21

Philadelphia Cartouche
22–59

Philadelphia Applied Pierced Shell Medallion 60–71

Philadelphia Applied Pierced Vine 72–85

Ogee Bracket Feet: Standard and Blocked 86–101

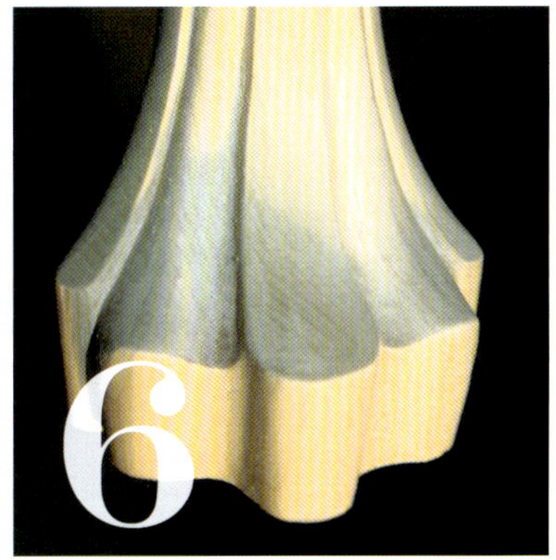

Triffid Foot
102–109

Philadelphia Chippendale Chair Carved Crest Rail
110–123

Philadelphia Chippendale Chair Pierced and Carved Back Splat 124–133

John Goddard Open Talon Ball and Claw Foot
134–159

INTRODUCTION

The projects in this book complement and add to those I presented in my first book, *Carving 18th Century American Furniture Elements*. Choosing the projects was somewhat arbitrary, but I picked ones that I thought were stylistically significant and important for a large variety of pieces. Most of them are representative of elements found on many pieces. A couple of them—the blocked ogee bracket foot and the Goddard open talon foot—are less common, but stylistically important and iconic. The cartouche is one of the pinnacles of eighteenth-century furniture embellishment and I included it because it is artistically stunning, technically challenging, and visually impressive.

The techniques used to carve the various elements can be readily adapted to other designs and furniture pieces. The swan neck molding is common to countless case pieces and it is one of the defining motifs of the period. While there is a wide variety of designs for applied, pierced carvings, the techniques to implement them are common. The examples I chose are complex enough to be representative of the most ambitious designs available. The crest rail and back splat are part of one of the most elaborate and elegant Philadelphia chairs ever made. The triffid foot, while less complex, is nonetheless elegant and representative of earlier eighteenth-century designs.

As with my first book, it is my intent to describe complex projects in a step-by-step process that the diligent reader can understand and implement. These projects are a representative sample of very high style eighteenth-century furniture motifs. Your successful completion of them will raise your skill level beyond what you might have imagined, and will be a source of pride for you and a legacy for generations to come.

SWAN NECK MOLDING

A swan (or goose) neck molding is the wide, extra thick, S-shaped, profiled element that is attached to the upper perimeter of the scroll board of a high chest or tall case clock. This molding adds a third dimension that is both dramatic and bold and immediately draws one's eye. It is one of the iconic elements that characterize the finest eighteenth-century pieces. In most cases the profiled surface is left bare, but occasionally additional elements are carved on the shaped profile. This treatment is rare and is only found on a few of the best of the best.

Many times the swan neck terminates at the top in a circular cylinder that will then have a carved rosette attached. The cylinder may or may not be integral with the swan neck. This is typical of furniture from Philadelphia. In other cases it will not hold a rosette and simply returns at both the top and bottom. Some Newport case work illustrates this form. Figures 1-1 and 1-2 show two typical examples.

This chapter will describe how to visualize, lay out, and execute this classic motif. The example here is sized for a tall case clock and the circular cylinder is integral with the molding. This is slightly more complex than if the cylinder was separate, so if you can do this one you can carve any molding from any piece of eighteenth-century furniture.

The first step to carving a swan neck molding is to visualize how the profile will be shaped on a straight section. Once you understand how to carve the profile along a straight line, it is a small step to carve that same profile along a curved one.

To begin, look at how to conceptually extract the profile from a blank of wood. Figure 1-3 shows a sequence of steps that will shape the given profile from a square. This profile will be formed after removing five sections of wood. The strategy is to make a stair step that isolates the ogee and the thumbnail—that is, the rounded corner. Next remove the cove section, leaving a small fillet on both top and bottom. Finally, round the corner and shape the ogee.

There are several ways to make these cuts on a straight section. Traditionally these would have been made with wooden molding planes of various shapes both concave and convex. They could also be approximated with power tools and cleaned up with planes and scrapers. I choose to carve them with traditional carving tools and smooth them with files and scrapers. This last method is easily adaptable to curved lines, whereas the other two have significant limitations when the line is not straight. It is the hand-carved method that I am going to describe in this chapter.

Figure 1-1.

Figure 1-2.

MOLDING PROFILE PROGRESSION

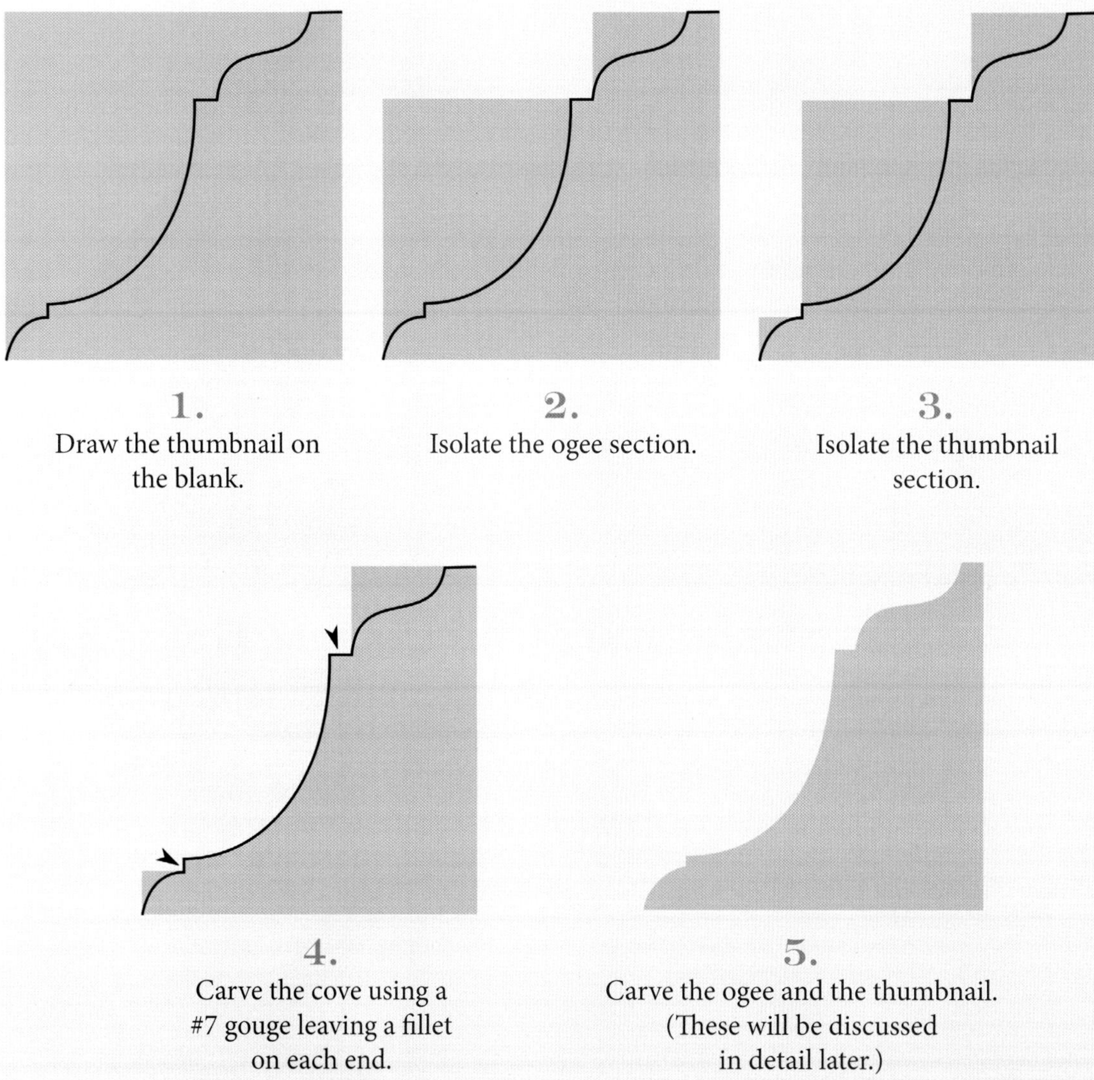

Figure 1-3. Conceptual steps to extract the molding from rectangular section of wood.

SWAN NECK TEMPLATE AND MOLDING PROFILE

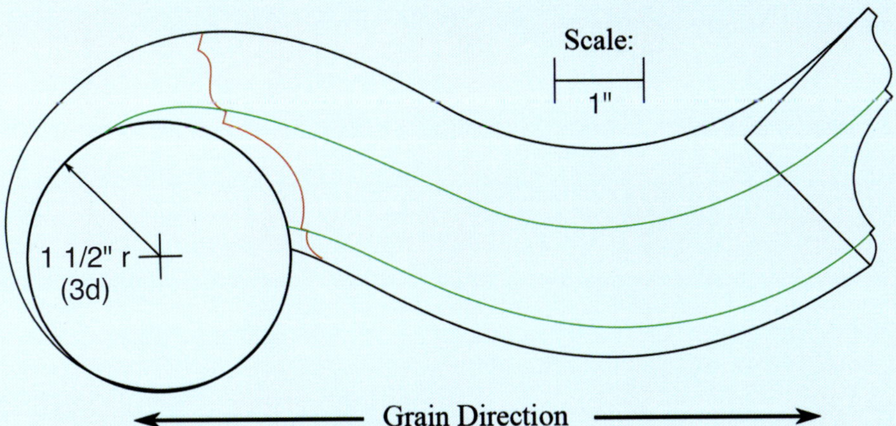

This template needs to be scaled by a factor of 2.5 to reach full scale. As a check, the circle should be 3" in diameter. Also note that this template is drawn for a specific clock and is used to illustrate the techniques to carve the molding. In general it will not fit any other project without modification. To adapt this to some other project, first determine the shape of the scroll board. Then draw the swan neck molding from the scroll board. Next draw the molding profile that will be carved along the curve of the swan neck on the bottom end of the blank. Use the techniques in this chapter to carve the shape.

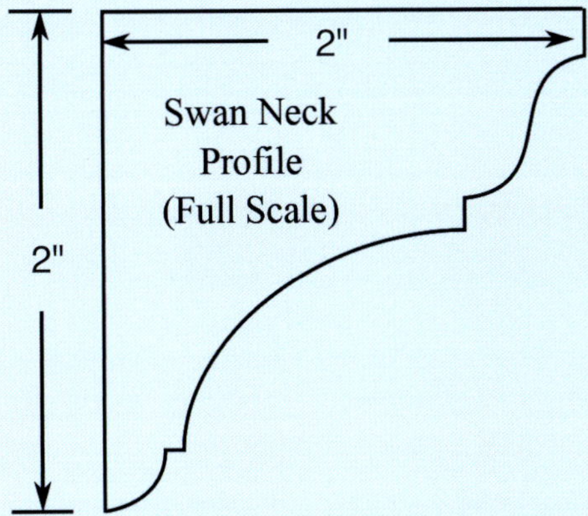

Full scale molding profile. Draw the profile on the bottom end of the swan neck blank.

Figure 1-4. The two templates needed for the swan neck molding.

SWAN NECK MOLDING

Start by scaling and tracing the swan neck template on a 2"-thick piece of wood with the grain oriented as shown in figure 1-4. This orientation will be the strongest structurally. Figure 1-5 shows this on the wood. Trace the template with a relatively thick pencil line and cut to the outside of that line. This will oversize the blank just enough so that there is extra material that will be removed when the molding is attached to the scroll board and the two are smoothed together. Also mark the center of the circular cylinder with an awl or other pointed tool. This will be used later as part of the layout process. Next draw the molding profile from figure 1-3 on the bottom end. This profile is the main guide from which all the layout lines will be drawn. The orientation of the profile is important, since there is a top and a bottom. In this case, the ogee is at the top of the molding and the thumbnail is at the bottom. Figure 1-6 shows the profile properly oriented on the blank. Now cut out the swan neck shape on the band saw. Figure 1-7 shows the results.

The next step is to draw a layout line on the top and one on the side that will help carry the profile along the curve of the swan neck. Recall from the conceptualized drawings that the first cut will isolate the ogee at the top. Figure 1-8 shows the rectangle that defines the first cut. On the top, transfer the line that isolates the ogee. With your finger held against the top edge as a guide, hold the pencil the required distance from the edge and draw a line parallel to the top edge. Figure 1-9 shows the technique. Next use a marking gauge to score a line on the side that is the bottom of the ogee. This is shown in figure 1-10. Finally, use a compass to draw a 3" circle centered at the point marked from the template. This will become the circular cylinder to which a rosette will eventually be attached. Figure 1-11 shows the layout complete. Now remove this S-shaped, rectangular cross section from the bottom edge up to the circle.

Clamp the blank to a flat surface as shown in figure 1-12 and start to set in along the S-curve on the top. These cuts should be 90° to the top surface. A #2 12 mm carving tool is a good choice for the flatter portion of the curve at the bottom and a #3 12 mm tool is good for the tighter curve closer to the circle and for the circle itself. Walk the #2 chisel along the S-curve, changing the orientation of the tool when the S changes concavity and blending it into the #3 as the circle approaches. Also walk the #3 along the portion of the circle that is currently part of the blank. Figure 1-13 shows the set-in lines on the top surface.

Figure 1-5. The swan neck template transferred to the blank. Note the grain direction is along the line of the molding.

Figure 1-6. Draw the depth profile on the bottom end of the blank.

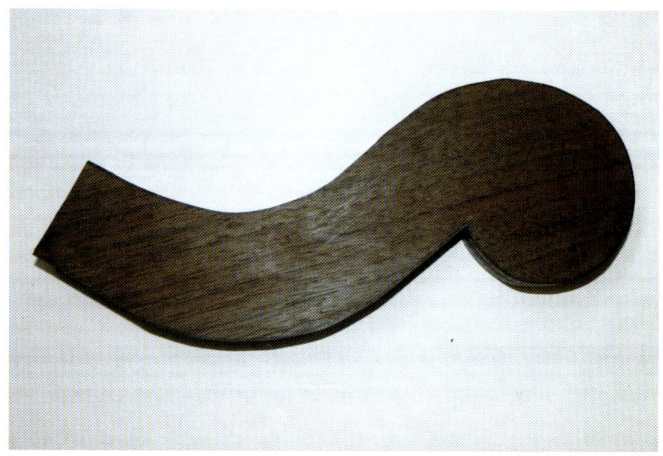

Figure 1-7. The front profile is cut with a band saw.

Figure 1-8. The first rectangular section to be removed.

Figure 1-11. The initial layout line following the S-curve.

Figure 1-9. Use your finger as a guide to transfer the line along the S-shape.

Figure 1-10. Use a marking gauge to transfer this line.

Figure 1-12. Set in using a gouge that matches the curve locally.

The next step is to remove the wood below the set in line down to the scored line on the bottom edge and the outside of the circle. Figure 1-14 shows the area to be removed in yellow. Start by carving a deep trough near the S-curve. Stay a little distance away from the line. I used a #9 15 mm gouge for this, but a narrower #9 or an equivalent #8 would accomplish the same thing. The goal is to isolate the line while making it easy to remove the waste without impacting the line. This will make it easier to pare to the line because there will be less resistance for the chisel. Figure 1-15 shows this step.

Now use a wider #7 gouge to quickly remove the waste material. Figures 1-16 and 1-17 show early and intermediate progress, respectively. I used a #7 20 mm for this operation, but a #5 of medium width would work, too. Depending on the wood species, this work will be harder or easier. This example is in relatively hard walnut, so I used a mallet to help drive the gouge. It is a lot easier on the hand and there is less chance of an error with a mallet. The harder the wood, the harder one has to push. The harder one pushes, the greater the chance of slippage and thus an error. There is no right way to do this and there are many that will work fine. The main thing to remember is to know what result you are trying to achieve and use the tools that you have to accomplish it. A gouge with a little bit of a curve will prevent the edges from catching and a wider one will remove material quicker. Next, deepen the trough near the S-curve and remove the waste in the same manner. Continue in this fashion until just proud of the horizontal line. Figure 1-18 shows the intended result.

The remaining work is to pare to the lines around the circle, along the S-curve and flush with the horizontal ledge. Because most of the waste material has been removed, there should not be a lot of resistance to the remaining cuts. Use a ½" flat chisel with the bevel down to lower the area right next to the S-curve. Because this line has been set in, the material will simply fall away. Figure 1-19 shows the technique and some early progress. With the same flat chisel, knock off the edges of the waste material near the circular arc. This is shown in figure 1-20. Finally, with ¾" flat chisel registered in the score line on the bottom edge, pare a horizontal shelf into the S-curve and circular arc. See figure 1-21 for the technique and early progress. Don't try to make complete cuts during any of these stages; remove as much as comes off easily and then repeat the steps. That is, set in deeper along the perimeter lines and then remove the waste down to the new depth.

Figure 1-13. The initial set-in is complete.

Figure 1-14. Remove the yellow section.

Figure 1-15. With a #9 15 mm gouge, carve a trough parallel but a short distance away from the line.

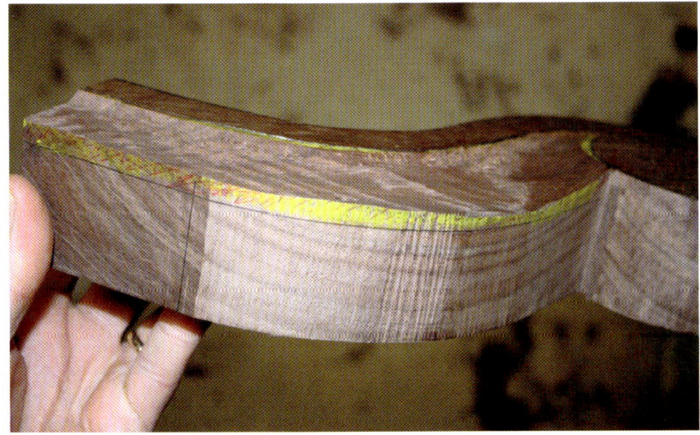

Figure 1-16. Use a #7 20 mm gouge to remove the waste as quickly as possible. Early progress.

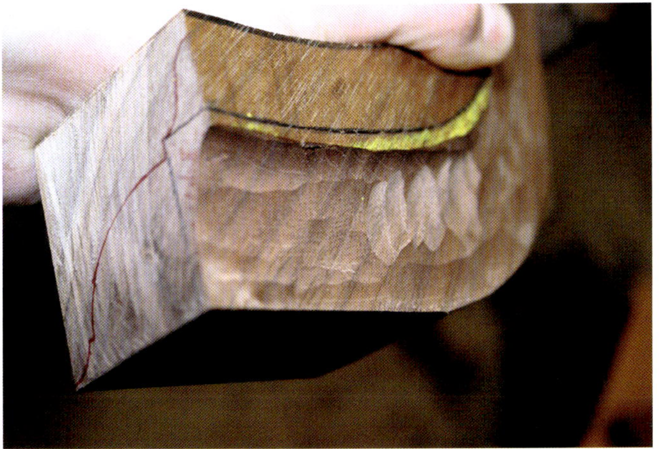

Figure 1-17. Waste removal—intermediate progress.

Figure 1-18. Waste removal—late progress. Deepen the #9 cut and remove more with the #7.

Figure 1-19. Use a flat chisel to remove the little bit of material next to the line.

Figure 1-20. Use the flat chisel to remove material next to the circle.

Figure 1-21. Use a ¾" flat chisel to form the shelf. Use the score line to register the chisel.

After a couple of iterations, progress will look like that illustrated in Figure 1-22. Note that there is more waste material in the corner between the S-curve and the horizontal the closer one gets to the intersection. To make the paring easier here, use a #9 10 mm gouge to remove the bulk of the waste, as also shown in Figure 1-22. Now pare down further and repeat the process until the two surfaces meet at a right angle.

The area where the S-curve meets the circular arc is pretty tight quarters. Because it is more difficult to get tools in here, it will not be as easy to clean this area out. In addition, smaller tools are needed to fit into the tighter spaces. I used a #1 3 mm skew chisel to remove the waste material up to the S-curve. As before, alternate between setting in along the perimeter line and removing the waste up to it. Figure 1-23 shows the technique and intermediate results.

Now check to see that the shelf is parallel to the top. Use a square as shown in figure 1-24 to see if the shelf is horizontal. If it isn't, remove material as needed until the shelf is square to its adjacent face. Figure 1-25 shows this operation complete.

The next step is to remove the vertical rectangle that will isolate the thumbnail along the bottom edge. This is the second step in the conceptual sequence. Use the same layout techniques as before. Use your finger as a guide to draw a line parallel to the bottom edge ¼" in on the top of the newly created shelf. Use a marking gauge set to ¼" to score a line along the S-curve on the bottom edge. Figure 1-26 shows these lines.

Set in along the S-curve on the shelf similar to the previous section. Be careful here and don't push or hit the chisel too hard because the cut is ¼" from the edge and could break off. Use a knife to deepen the scored line on the bottom edge. With the blank in a vise as shown in figure 1-27 start to remove the waste using a ½" flat chisel. Iteratively deepen the perimeter lines and remove the waste until complete. I found that, for the most part, cutting across the grain worked better than cutting with it. What will ultimately be the best depends on the specific piece of wood and the grain direction. Figures 1-28 and 1-29 show early and intermediate progress, respectively, and figure 1-30 shows the operation complete. Compare progress so far with the conceptual drawings.

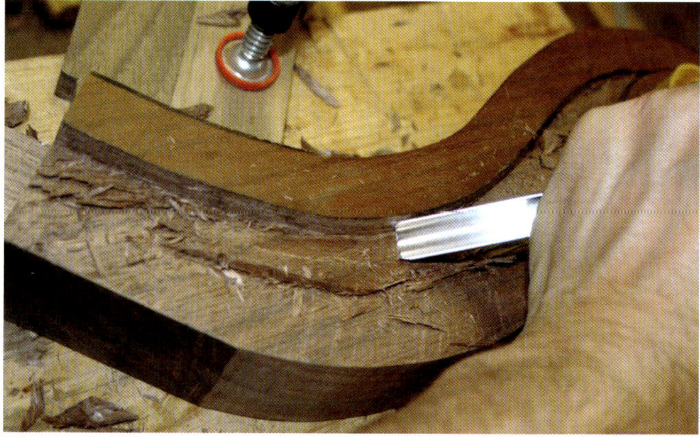

Figure 1-22. Use a #9 10 mm gouge to remove most of the waste along the intersection line.

Figure 1-23. Use a #1 3 mm skew chisel near the circle.

Figure 1-24. Use a square to check that the shelf is square to the bottom edge. A little more to do.

Figure 1-25. The ogee section is now isolated along the entire S-curve.

Figure 1-26. Layout lines for removing the rectangle that will isolate the thumbnail.

Figure 1-27. Early progress near the button cylinder.

Figure 1-28. Early progress cutting across the grain.

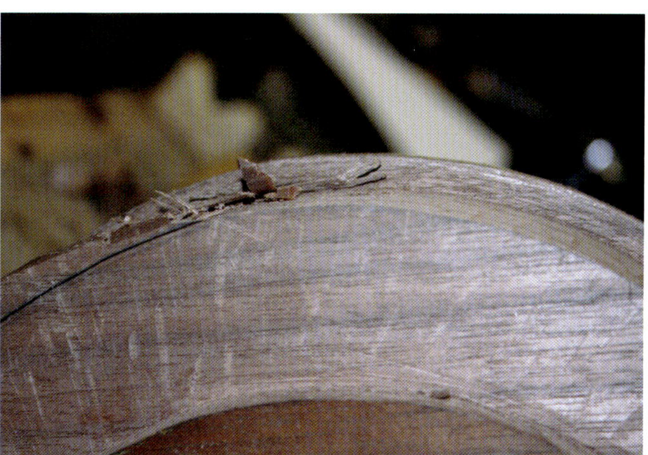
Figure 1-29. Intermediate progress cutting across the grain.

Figure 1-30. The thumbnail section is now isolated.

Next remove the coved portion of the stair step. A fillet is needed on both top and bottom to separate the cove from the thumbnail and the ogee. Because the fillet is narrow on the horizontal surface, make several tick marks along the line of the S-curve as shown in figure 1-31. Connect these tick marks to get the desired curve. Use a marking gauge referenced from the top shelf to score a line on the bottom edge. These lines are positioned as defined by the profile drawn on the end. Figure 1-32 shows these lines.

There is a lot of wood to remove here, so be aggressive in the beginning. I mostly used a #7 20 mm gouge with a mallet to hog out the majority of the waste. A flat chisel could also be used in the beginning until the corner is removed. After that the gouge will be a better choice. Figure 1-33 shows intermediate progress and figure 1-34 shows later progress. Note how the line of intersection between the cove and the circular cylinder wraps around the cylinder as the coved surface moves toward the top. Be careful to keep the wall of the cylinder perpendicular to the top. Until most of the waste is removed, stay away from the cylinder wall a little bit and pare to it later.

With the #7 20 mm gouge, carve as close to the lines as possible. Don't take too much wood off at any one time and slide the gouge along a skewed line relative to the cove in a slicing motion. This will give greater control and nicer cuts. Although it is a lot of work, most of the cove is relatively straightforward.

Cutting the cove near the cylinder is more tricky. You will have to use a flatter gouge than the #7 because the edges of the steeper chisel will prevent you from getting close enough. With a #5 12 mm gouge, deepen the center of the cove into the wall of the cylinder. Keep the cutting edge of the chisel parallel to the cove/cylinder intersection line as you deepen the curve. Figure 1-35 shows the technique. Cut across the grain from the top to the center and from the bottom up until the curve blends with the other portion of the cove and it has a pleasing look. Use the smaller skewed chisel in the narrowest portion. Don't worry about getting this section perfect at this point. It will be revisited later when the ogee material is removed. Then there will be a little more room to maneuver the tools.

At this point the cove is mostly shaped, but it has many small facets that need to be blended. I use a French curved scraper to do most of the smoothing and blending. Use various portions of the scraper to match the cove along the length of the S-curve and iteratively cut to the pencil lines that delineate the curve. Figure 1-36 shows the technique and the desired result. When the blending is done, the cove is complete. Figure 1-37 shows the completed cove with the two fillets and the isolated blocks that will become the ogee and thumbnail.

Figure 1-31. The fillet is ⅛" wide. Connect the tick marks to form the curve.

Figure 1-32. The limits of the cove are defined.

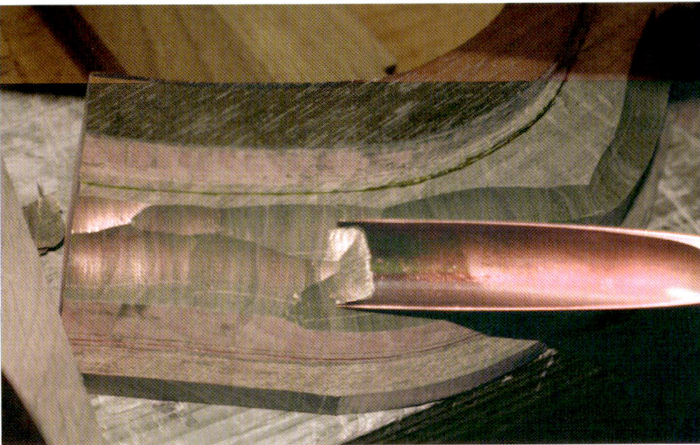

Figure 1-33. Use a big gouge to remove wood quickly.

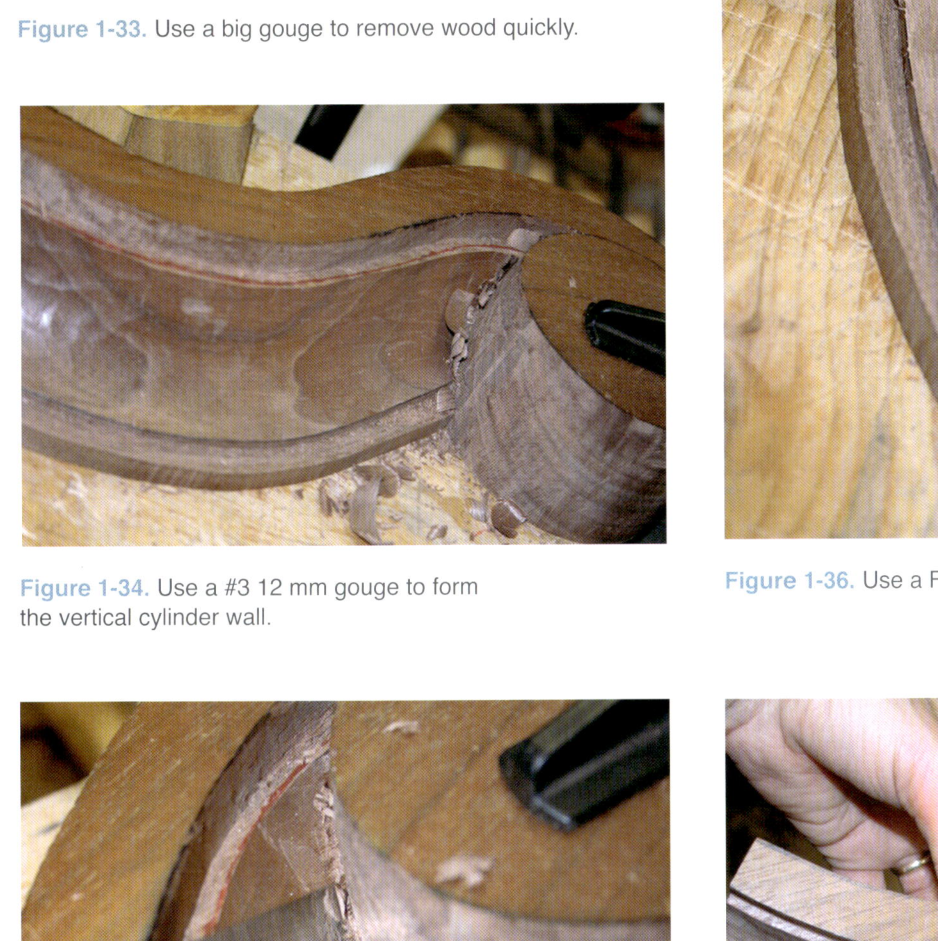

Figure 1-34. Use a #3 12 mm gouge to form the vertical cylinder wall.

Figure 1-35. Use a #5 12 mm gouge to clean up near the cylinder wall.

Figure 1-36. Use a French curved scraper to blend the facets.

Figure 1-37. The cove is now complete.

SWAN NECK MOLDING

Before shaping the ogee and thumbnail elements, consider the strategy that will be used. The thumbnail will be shaped by first beveling the corner at 45° and then beveling between adjacent center points of the resulting three flat surfaces. This leaves a four-sided polygonal approximation of the curve. The polygon will be smoothed with a file, scraper, and sand paper to the final curve. Figure 1-38 shows the progression.

With your finger as a guide, draw a line on each face of the square at the halfway point. Measure this by eye. Figure 1-39 shows the top line and the corner to be removed. Use a ½" flat chisel to bevel between these two lines along the path of the S-curve. Figure 1-40 shows the desired result. These don't have to be perfect because this is just an approximation and any defects will be cleaned up later. With the same flat chisel, connect the center points of two adjacent segments with another bevel. You don't have to draw lines for this; your eye will be good enough. Figure 1-41 shows this step and figure 1-42 shows the result.

Now use a small, flat file to round over the bottom portion of the curve. Figure 1-43 shows the technique and the result. Continue to use a file to blend the flat segments into a smooth curve. I have a bent file that works well for this operation, but the small flat one will work too. Finally, I use a flat scraper or a flat chisel as a scraper to shape the curve at the intersection with the fillet. It is hard to get right up to the fillet line with anything other that a flat scraper. If needed I will use a small piece of 120-grit sandpaper with my thumb as a backing for final shaping. Use your eye to look for unblended areas and any other irregularities. You can also use your finger to feel for any areas that need a little more smoothing.

THUMBNAIL APPROXIMATION PROGRESSION

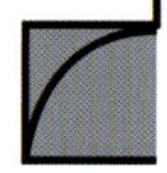

1\.
Draw the thumbnail on the blank.

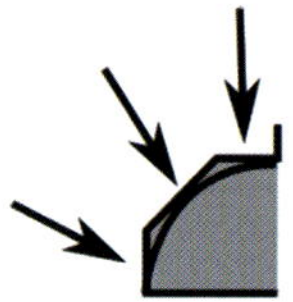

2\.
Bevel the corner 45°.

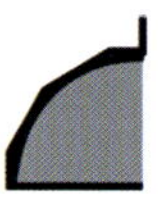

3\.
Bevel between adjacent center points as indicated by the arrows.

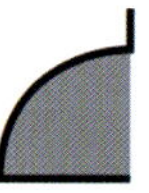

4\.
Clean up the remaining facets with scrapers, files, and sandpaper.

Figure 1-38. The rounded thumbnail is first approximated as a series of bevels using a flat chisel and then the small remaining ridges are filed smooth.

Figure 1-39. Use your finger as a guide to draw this line along the S-curve.

Figure 1-40. Bevel the corner between the two layout lines along the S-curve.

Figure 1-41. Begin the secondary bevel in approximating the thumbnail.

Figure 1-42. The secondary bevels are complete.

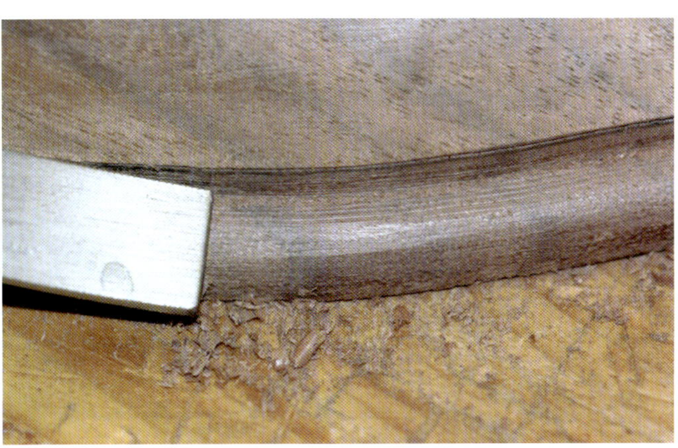

Figure 1-43. Use a bent file to blend the upper facets. The thumbnail is now complete.

Figure 1-44. The two layout lines on the top of the ogee segment.

SWAN NECK MOLDING

The ogee at the top is the last remaining element. See Figure 1-45 for a conceptual, sequential progression of the necessary steps. As before, use your finger as a guide to draw two lines parallel to the S-curve on the top flat surface. The upper one defines the flat area at the very top of the completed molding and the second one is between the first line and the lower edge of the segment, closer to the lower edge. Note how these lines blend into the circular cylinder. The upper one curves quite far around the cylinder and tapers into the perimeter of the circle. The lower one remains parallel to the upper one until it terminates into the circle.

Figure 1-44 shows both of these lines. Using the same technique, draw a line about two-thirds of the way down on the adjacent face. Figure 1-46 shows this line. Note that these guidelines are not precise, so don't worry if they are not perfect. They are determined by the final profile and are used to approximate it.

Analogous to the thumbnail, use a flat chisel to create a bevel between the two layout lines. Figure 1-47 shows this result. Now use a #9 13 mm gouge to carve the concave portion of the ogee at the top. Figure 1-48 shows early progress and figure 1-49 shows the operation mostly complete. As this concave cut merges into the cylinder, you will have to roll the gouge to use less and less of the cutting edge to avoid the chisel point from hitting the cylinder wall. You can also use a flatter gouge like a #3 or #5 12 mm gouge across the grain to approximate the curve. Let your eye tell you when there is enough depth to the curve.

The bottom portion of the ogee is shaped just like the thumbnail. Use the flat chisel to approximate it and then use the file and straight scraper to blend the facets. Finally, use scrapers to bring the top concave portion right to the line and to blend the transition between the concave and convex portions. I have a series of semi-circular scrapers that work very well for this. Figure 1-50 shows the technique. Figure 1-51 shows the completed swan neck molding. It is now ready to be fixed to the scroll board and joined to its return molding.

OGEE CURVE APPROXIMATION PROGRESSION

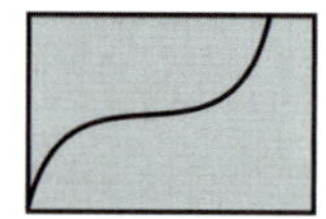

1.
Draw the ogee curve on the blank.

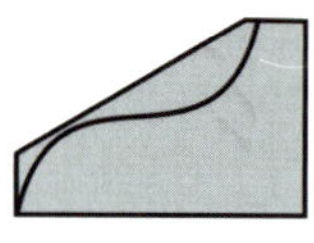

2.
Bevel the corner with a flat chisel.

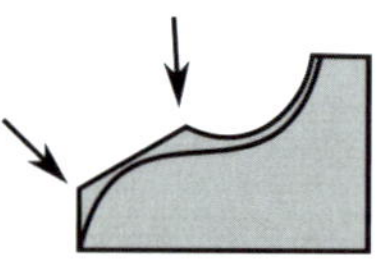

3.
Use #9 15 mm gouge. A #8 will also work.

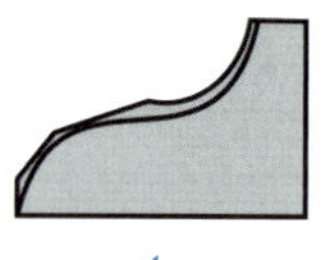

4.
Bevel the two corners.

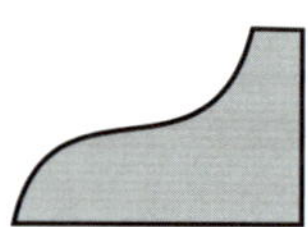

5.
Clean up with chisels, scrapers, files, and sandpaper.

Figure 1-45. The ogee is approximated first and then refined.

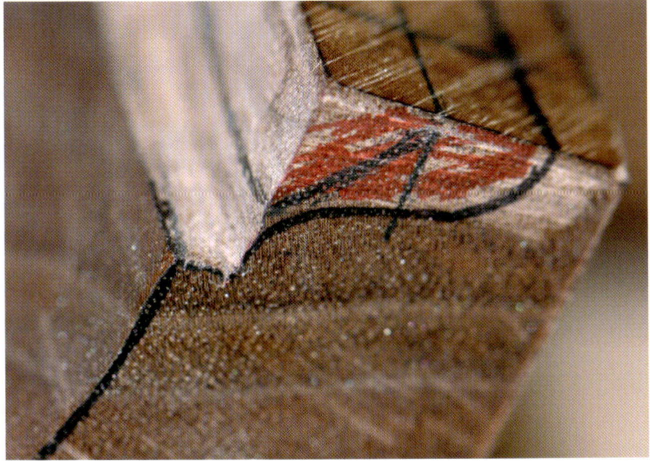

Figure 1-46. The layout line for the convex portion of the ogee is two-thirds of the way down from the top.

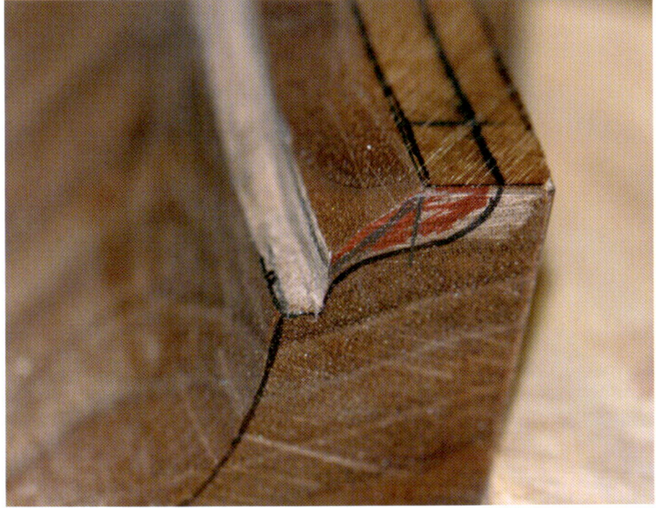

Figure 1-47. Use a flat chisel to remove the corner between the layout lines.

Figure 1-48. Use a #9 13 mm gouge to carve the concave portion of the ogee. Carve close to the line.

Figure 1-49. The carved portion of the ogee is complete. Final cleanup is done with files and scrapers.

Figure 1-50. Use the semi-circular scrapers to bring the concave portion of the ogee to the line.

Figure 1-51. The completed swan neck molding.

PHILADELPHIA CARTOUCHE

A carved cartouche was used as the central pediment on only the finest eighteenth-century Philadelphia tall case furniture. Only a few tall case clocks and high chests were adorned with this elaborate element. A cartouche would look out of place on an unembellished case, as would a top hat on a person dressed in casual clothes. So typically the case itself would be highly ornate.

Figure 2-1.

A cartouche is one of the most elaborate and detailed carved elements used during the period. Its shape and accentuated third dimension are both dramatic and refined. Figures 2-1 and 2-2 show two typical examples.

The cartouche that I am going to describe in this chapter is a uniquely Philadelphia design with the characteristic "peanut" in the center. It is sized to fit a tall case clock. There are several pictures at the end of this chapter that show a completed cartouche from various angles. It is difficult to describe every detail and nuance, so study these pictures to get an overall feel for the shape and refer to them throughout the project.

This cartouche is extracted from a block of 12/4 stock 7" wide by 13½" high. The element itself only needs 6/4 of stock, but the extra thickness is desirable so that the remaining "cradle" can be used to help with clamping. In order not to waste good wood, a piece of scrap wood can be glued to the back of a 6/4 block to get the extra thickness. The thickness doesn't have to be 4", but make sure there is enough to allow for a sufficiently sturdy "cradle."

Figure 2-2. Partial clock bonnet. This cartouche is the one described in this chapter.

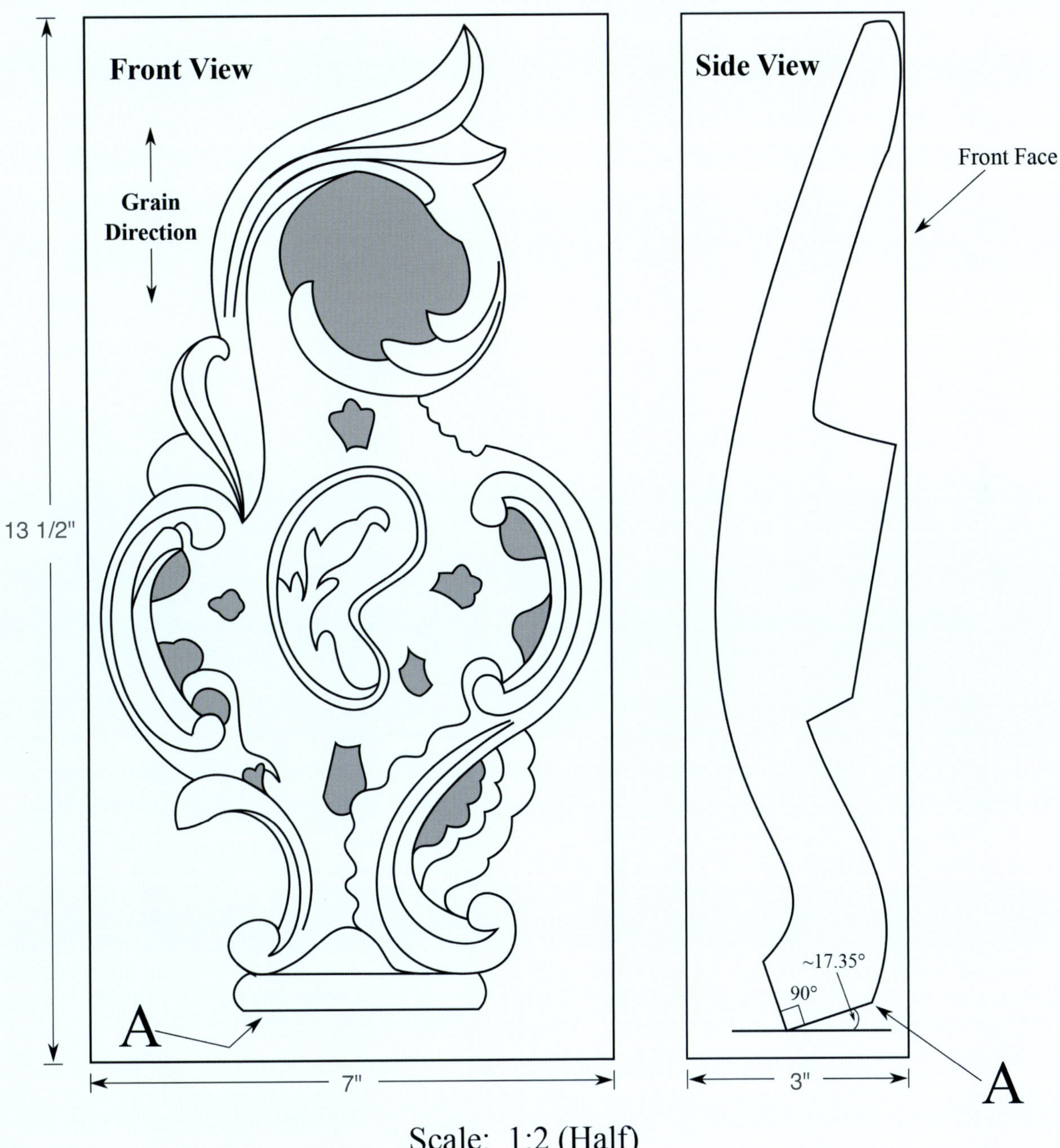

Figure 2-3. This is a half-scale drawing. The side and front views align along the point labeled "A" in the side view with the line labeled "A" in the front view. Note also the angle that the side view makes with the horizontal. This angle cants the cartouche forward when it is in place, and is approximate. Use a bevel gauge to set and mark the angle. The shaded portions in the front view are cut out. The cartouche blank is 12/4 (3") stock 7" wide by 13½" tall. When cutting the side view profile, keep the back cutout portion as a carving "cradle." This will be used to support and clamp the cartouche while carving.

PHILADELPHIA CARTOUCHE

First make a template from the side view profile shown in figure 2-3 and transfer it to the blank as shown in figure 2-4. Note the right angle between the bottom and the back. This is important so that it will mount properly on the top of the case. When in place, the cartouche will sit with its bottom parallel to the floor and leaning forward. This is because it is typically 7'-8' off the ground and it is more visible in this position when viewed from below.

With a hand saw, cut along the bottom line to remove the lower corner. Use a hand plane and straight edge to make the bottom a flat surface. If this surface is not flat, it will not seat well when in place and an unsightly gap may occur. Figure 2-5 shows what to strive for.

Next use a square referenced from the bottom to verify that the back is at a right angle. Make adjustments from the template as necessary to get a square corner. See figure 2-6. Now use a band saw to cut along the back line. To save the waste for the "cradle," saw the back from the bottom up to the transition point as shown in figure 2-7. Now back out from the cut and saw from the top. Figure 2-8 shows the result. Finally, verify that the back and bottom are square to each other as shown in figure 2-9 and make any adjustments if they are not.

Figure 2-4. Transfer the side profile to the edge of the blank. Leave enough material on the back to use as a carving cradle.

Figure 2-5. Flatten the base face. When in place, the cartouche sits on this surface.

Figure 2-6. Use the bottom face as a reference to square up the back surface.

Figure 2-7. To preserve the cradle, cut along the back face first. Back out of the cut without making the turn.

Figure 2-8. Cut from the top along the back face and exit into the first cut.

Figure 2-9. Check that the back and bottom surfaces are square to each other.

Before cutting the front portion of the side profile, transfer the template made from the front profile in figure 2-3 to the front of the blank. Take care that the "peanut" aligns with the central angled section. The bottom should also align. Figure 2-10 shows the placement. Now use a band saw to cut along the front portion of the side profile. Do this in three cuts and save the waste sections because they have the front profile that is going to be needed later. Figure 2-11 shows progress and figure 2-12 shows the operation complete.

Now use some double stick tape to reattach the front waste pieces. See figure 2-13. With the front waste pieces attached and sitting in the cradle, cut out the front profile using a band saw. None of the waste pieces from this operation are needed again, so don't worry about preserving them. Make stop cuts as needed to assist in cutting to the profile line. Figure 2-14 shows the results of this step.

There are several piercings in this cartouche. To help position these and to make carving around them easier, drill some holes in the center of each pierced area. Drill multiple holes in the top plume area since this whole section will be gone. A ¼" drill should work well for this. Figure 2-15 shows the holes drilled.

Remove the front waste pieces and use the front template to locate the peanut on the angled central section as shown in figure 2-16. On the side edge draw a line 1" from the bottom in the angled central area. This line more or less connects the surface below and above the central area. This line will be used as the target depth in the next step when excavating the peanut. Figure 2-17 shows this line. At this point the cartouche is roughed out and ready for carving.

Before I begin carving, I want to make a few observations about the strategy to keep in mind throughout. The most important feature to a successful cartouche is to get the shape correct. By this I mean the contoured high and low areas at the proper depth relative to each other. Once the shape and levels are correct, the detail is relatively easy. However, if the levels are not correct it will be impossible to get the details to look good relative to each other. So don't think about the details until the levels are correct. Another way to think about this is to look at a finished one and visualize what would be the minimum surface that just envelops the detail. That is the surface you are trying to achieve. If you continually come back to this thought and correct the surface before adding the detail, you will end up with a much better result.

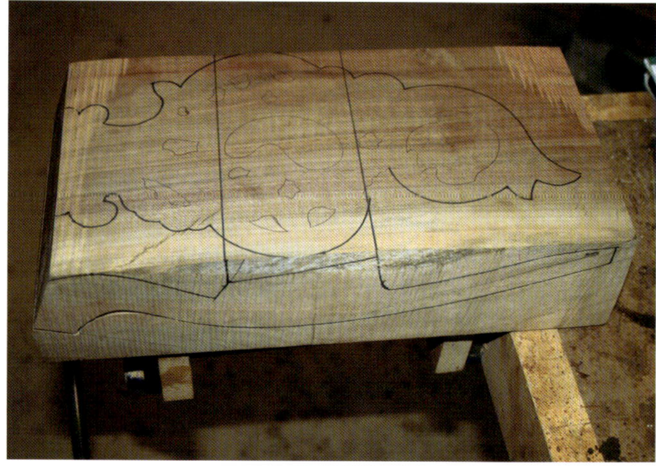

Figure 2-10. Draw the front profile on the front of the blank. Make sure to align the front profile with side points as shown.

Figure 2-11. Cut the front portion of the side profile. Save the waste pieces because they will be used to cut the front profile.

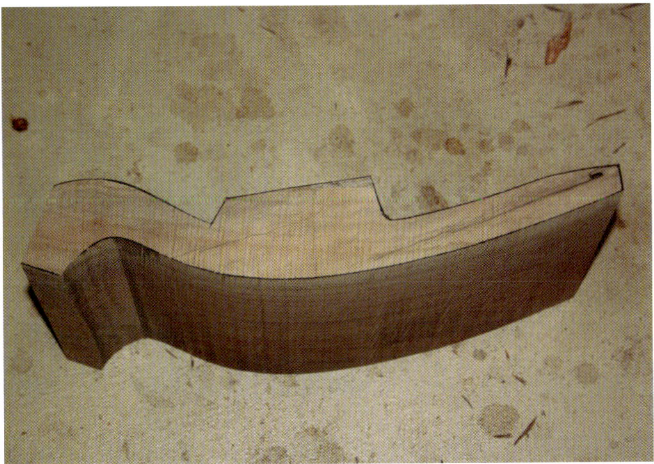

Figure 2-12. The cartouche blank after the side profiles are cut.

Figure 2-13. Attach the front waste pieces with double stick tape.

Figure 2-14. Use a band saw to cut the front profile. None of these waste pieces are needed, so make as many stop cuts as necessary to easily follow the line.

Figure 2-15. Drill holes in the pierced areas. Note that several holes are drilled in the plume area. This will make it easier to remove this section later.

Figure 2-16. Use the front template to locate the peanut.

Figure 2-17. Draw a line 1" from the bottom face.

Another important observation is that until the shape and levels are correct, individual areas will be worked iteratively. By this I mean that one area will be refined some, but not to completion, and then another area will be worked. When all, or most, areas are refined to some extent, another pass will be made to move closer to the final shape. This process continues until the final shape is achieved.

Finally, although I am trying to provide a detailed and complete description of how to carve this object, there is not an exact step-by-step method that guarantees perfection. This is way too complicated for that. So visual judgment is required at all times. If something doesn't look good, it probably isn't and adjustments will be needed. This mostly translates to removing more wood. It is highly unlikely that you will take off too much wood. Within reason "deeper is better."

Use the cradle to support the cartouche blank as shown in figure 2-18. The first step is to isolate the peanut in the central section. At this point there is a lot of wood to remove, so try to do it as efficiently as possible by removing big chunks with a bigger tool. I iteratively used a #9 15 mm gouge and a #5 25 mm gouge. Use a mallet for much of this because it will give better control and be a lot easier on the hands. This is a lot of hard work, so be patient because it will take some time. Figures 2-19, 2-20 and 2-21 show a few progress stages.

At this point the perimeter of the peanut is close. Use a series of #9 gouges to carve near the "elbow" of the peanut. Start with wider ones at the top and switch to narrower ones as you blend the wall into the lower level. Figure 2-22 shows the peanut perimeter sufficiently excavated for now. The peanut should be at the top of a hill that slopes into the valley below.

Now isolate the peanut on top of a "butte." Start by drawing a line around the perimeter of the "peanut hill" ½" from the top. This is a little tricky because of the shape and access, but do the best that you can. I marked several points on the side ½" down and connected the dots. Figure 2-23 shows the result.

Use a flat chisel as shown in figure 2-24 to make a flat surface at the ½" line. Set in horizontally along the line and remove the wood on top of the line up to the peanut perimeter. Carve straight down from the peanut perimeter into the flat surface. Figure 2-25 shows early progress and figure 2-26 shows later progress. A flat chisel works well for the convex portions, but a #9 gouge is better for the narrow end and the concave elbow.

Figure 2-18. Clamp the cartouche blank and its cradle.

Figure 2-19. Start to isolate the peanut. Use a wide, medium-sweep gouge to remove material up to the peanut line and down to the 1" line on the side.

Figure 2-20. Progress on one side of the peanut.

Figure 2-21. Note how the sides of the peanut are sloped. This is okay for now. The goal is to roughly isolate the peanut.

Figure 2-22. Use a #9 gouge to work in the concave area.

Figure 2-23. The peanut sits on a "butte" and is ½" proud of the butte.

Figure 2-24. Form the flat portion of the butte. The goal will be to form a vertical wall that follows the peanut perimeter down to the top of the butte.

Figure 2-25. Progress establishing the peanut and the top of the butte.

Figure 2-26. More progress excavating the peanut.

Figure 2-27 shows the technique. Continue in this manner until the entire peanut is isolated with vertical walls into the flat surface at the ½" line. Figure 2-28 shows the result. Note that the ledge around the peanut is not equal. That's fine. I will take care of that in the next step.

Draw a line on the flat ledge ⅛" from the wall of the peanut around its perimeter. I used a ruler to mark several dots ⅛" away and then connected them. Figure 2-29 shows the technique and figure 2-30 shows the result.

Remove the material below the ledge and outside of the ⅛" line in a similar manner when first excavating the peanut. I used some gouges and a flat chisel to get the results. Figure 2-31 shows progress and figure 2-32 shows the step completed. At this point the peanut is sufficiently roughed out and sitting on a butte that is also good for now. No more work will be done on it until almost the end. The main reason for this is that the top of the peanut blank is the only flat spot on the top surface. This flat surface will be needed for clamping when work is done on the back later.

The next step is to isolate the central side C-scrolls. Start by drawing a line on the side as shown in figure 2-33. This line is about 5⁄16" up from the back in the center and connects to the top surface toward bottom.

Make a template for the right-hand C-scroll from figure 2-33 and align it as shown in figure 2-34. Transfer the lines as shown in figure 2-35. The right edge of the C-scroll is about ¼" from the edge and the piercings need to align with the drilled holes. With these constraints, position it as best as possible so that it looks good and balanced. This is one of the first of many judgments that will be made throughout this project. The goal is to be visually appealing as opposed to being a slave to some rigid measurement.

Figure 2-27. Use a #9 gouge around the bottom area.

Figure 2-28. The peanut is excavated and sitting on top of the butte. Its walls are pretty close to vertical.

Figure 2-29. The top of the butte will be trimmed to a width of ⅛" around the peanut. Use a ruler to make several marks at ⅛" from the base of the peanut.

Figure 2-30. Connect the dots to form the perimeter of the butte top.

Figure 2-31. Carve the sides of the butte to the line just drawn. The techniques are the same as used for roughing the peanut earlier.

Figure 2-32. The butte has been sufficiently reduced for now.

Figure 2-33. Draw a line 5⁄16" from the back face and connect it on the top face at the bottom as shown.

Figure 2-34. Make a partial template of the C-scroll element and position it around the holes.

Remove the material above the line on the side, while isolating the C-scrolls. As a first step toward this end, use a #9 15 mm gouge to cut a trough side to side as shown in figure 2-36. Stay below the C-scrolls on each side. As the trough deepens, remove the material from the bottom direction down to the lines drawn on the side edges. The goal is to connect the high portion at the bottom of the blank with a flowing surface that blends with the bottom of the trough and the base of the peanut butte. Figure 2-37 shows some progress. With the #9 15 mm gouge, begin to raise the C-scroll by cutting toward the side edge line. There is a lot more to do here, but work on another area now.

In order to get access to the top of the C-scrolls, work needs to be done to separate the plume. Start by drawing in the lines as shown in figure 2-38. I found it easiest to sketch these freehand, although you can make a template from figure 2-3 if it helps. The only real constraints here are that the bottom curve should blend nicely into the outer edge on the right and fit around the drilled holes.

Before raising the plume, remove the center section. Use a flat chisel to cut through the narrow bridges between adjacent holes. Make V-cuts as shown in figure 2-39. Remove material on both sides of the V to gain deeper access. Repeat this process until the center section can be removed. Figure 2-40 shows the results.

Now set in along the curve that defines the bottom of the plume and blend the surrounding surface into the bottom of the cut. Repeat these steps until the bottom of the cut is about 5⁄16" deep. The exact depth is not critical at this stage, but the point is that it should be pretty deep. Figure 2-41 shows progress after several iterations.

Figure 2-35. Transfer the C-scroll.

Figure 2-36. Cut a trough below the peanut.

Figure 2-37. Progress excavating the C-scroll. Blend the bottoms of the troughs.

Figure 2-39. Use a large V-tool to connect the drill holes in the plume interior.

Figure 2-38. Lines that determine the perimeter of the plume.

Figure 2-40. After a couple of iterations, the center piece is removed.

Figure 2-41. Set in along the bottom perimeter of the plume and form a vertical wall.

Return to the right C-scroll and work to implement the surface as shown in figure 2-42. Figure 2-42 shows the C-scroll and surrounding area completed. It is helpful to see the completed element so that you can better appreciate the steps to get there and make judgments along the way. The background on the inside of the C-scroll is a complex up and down surface that undulates around the pierced openings and blends smoothly into the base of the peanut butte.

Set in along the entire perimeter of the scroll. Form a vertical wall on the outside down to the line drawn previously on the side edge. On the inside dive into the stop cuts as shown in figure 2-43, leaving the areas labeled "A" high. Rough out the low portions using a #9 10 mm gouge. Note the rim around the lower portion of the scroll. This is labeled "B" in figure 2-43. Also set in along the perimeter of the piercings labeled "C" and cut down vertically ¼" or so. Don't go all the way, though, because that would be too difficult at this point and it will be worked on from the back later. Refine the rough surfaces in figure 2-43 until they get close to the finished version shown in figure 2-42. Radius scrapers of various sizes work well to blend the facets.

The C-scroll blank needs some shaping. Draw a line ¼" up from the outer ledge on the outside edge of the scroll. Use a flat chisel, rasp, and file to bevel the scroll down to the line just drawn, leaving the inside edge high. Figure 2-44 shows the result.

Next sketch in lines as shown in figure 2-45. Use a #7 6 mm gouge to set in along the circular portions of the scroll. Then use a #7 10 mm gouge to remove the material between the scroll ends up to the connecting line. Figure 2-46 shows early progress. Refer to the completed element in figure 2-42.

Now work on the left scroll. Draw the lines as shown in figure 2-47. I did not find a template as useful for the left C-scroll, so I drew it freehand. Note also the line on the side edge. This line is about ¼" from the back face and is the depth that the C-scroll will be raised. This line follows the contour of the back. Separate the top of the scroll from the area above with a #9 10 mm gouge. Blend the surface into the bottom of the gouge cut. Repeat this until the scroll is raised about ⅛".

Figure 2-42. This shows the completed C-scroll. Study the up-and-down surface on the interior of the scroll.

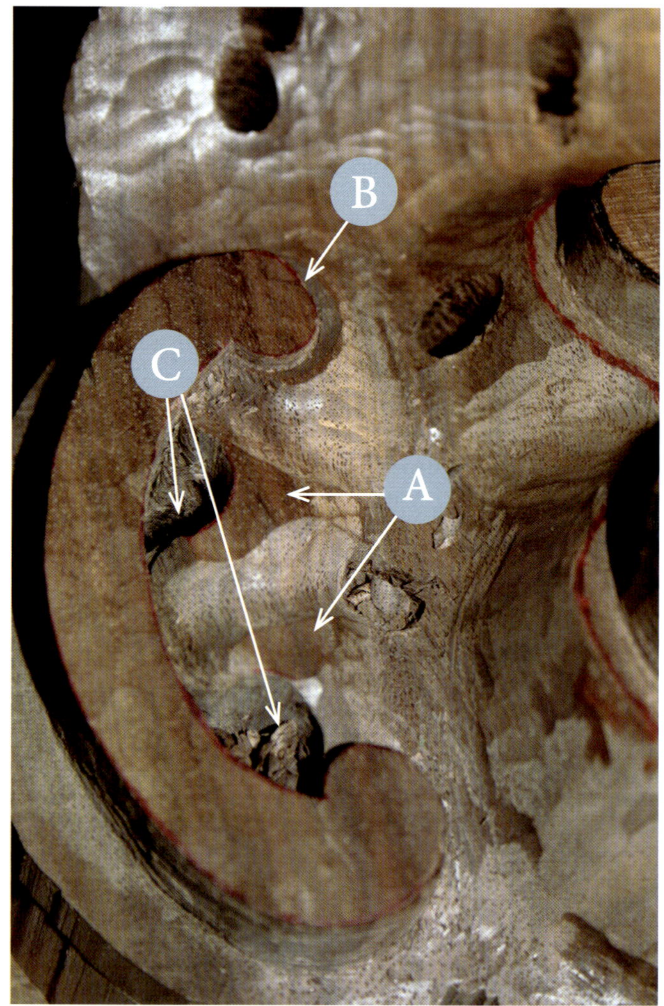

Figure 2-43. Note the various landmarks and compare this rough version with figure 2-42.

Figure 2-44. Angle the top surface of the C-scroll so that the thickness at the outer edge is approximately ¼".

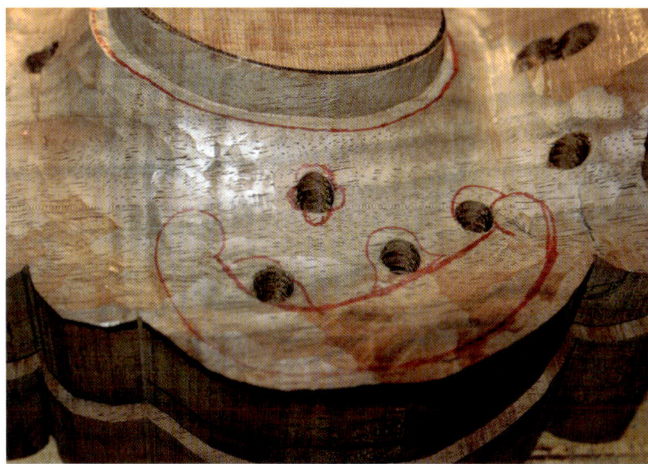

Figure 2-47. Draw the C-scroll on the other side.

Figure 2-45. These lines define the buttons on the ends of the scroll and the connecting edge.

Figure 2-48. The leaves on top of the left C-scroll are a little lower. Cut around the top of the scroll and lower the background into the cut. When the background is about ⅛" lower, draw in the leaves.

Figure 2-46. Remove the material between the scroll ends with a #7 10 mm gouge. (See right side of photo.)

Draw in the leaves above the C-scroll as shown in figure 2-48. Sketch these freehand and strive for smooth, flowing curves. Note how the leaf lines flow into the outside edge. Figure 2-49 shows this scroll and its surrounding area completed. Keep this image in mind as you work through the elements as described in the following steps.

Isolate the scroll and shape the piercing perimeters as on the right side. Figures 2-50 and 2-51 show early and advanced progress, respectively. Note that the leaves above the top and below the bottom of the scroll need to be outlined. Set in along these leaf lines using an appropriate gouge. A #7 of sufficient width should work well. Remove the material between the leaves and the scroll with a #1 1 mm chisel. The gaps between these elements are quite small and access is limited and difficult, so use whatever small tools you have to get a nice separation. Although this scroll is not complete, it is good enough for now.

Next separate the rope detail at the bottom from the main body of the cartouche. Draw a straight line on the bottom of the cartouche blank as shown in figure 2-52. It is ½" from the front face on the bottom edge. Use a straight edge and a knife to cut along this line. Figure 2-53 shows the technique. Draw two more straight lines on the front as shown in figure 2-54. The one labeled "A" connects the bottom of the scroll buttons and is also the top of the rope. The one labeled "B" is 1/16" up from the bottom face. Figure 2-55 shows a small rabbet that needs to be removed. Use a flat chisel to remove it. Figure 2-56 shows the technique. Figure 2-57 shows the rabbet complete.

Figure 2-49. Here is the completed left C-scroll area. Use this as a guide for forming the elements in this area.

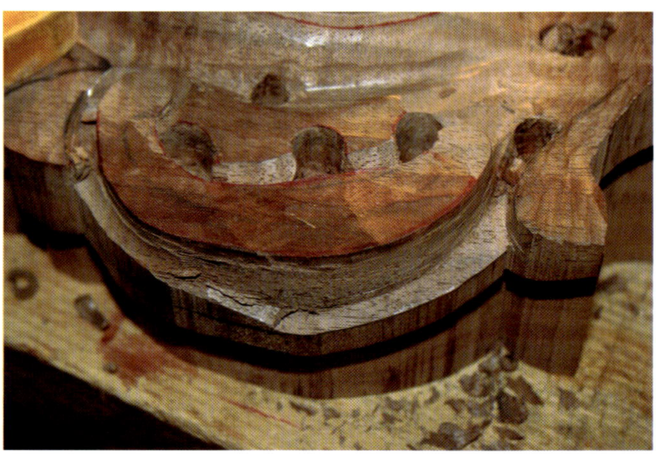

Figure 2-50. Separate the C-scroll from its surrounding elements. The height of the outside shelf is ¼" as on the other side. The elements on the bottom and top of the scroll are a little lower, but higher than the background. The interior is an up-and-down surface straddling the piercings.

Figure 2-51. The outside shelf is established and the C-scroll wall is vertical.

Figure 2-54. The top of the rope is defined by line "A." This connects the bottom of the buttons. Line "B" is 1⁄16" up from the bottom.

Figure 2-52. To isolate the rope detail at the bottom, draw a line across the bottom surface as shown (ignore the upper line).

Figure 2-55. Cut the rabbet that is defined by these lines. These are 1⁄16" and ½" lines that were just drawn.

Figure 2-53. Score the ½" line using a ruler and knife.

Figure 2-56. Use a flat chisel to cut the rabbet.

Figure 2-57 also shows how to separate the rope at the top. Set in along the line "A" in figure 2-57 and bevel into it from the bottom of the stop cut. Repeat until the depth is about 1⁄16". Use a #7 10 mm gouge with the bevel up to round over the surface of the rope. The rope detail will be added later.

Draw in lines as shown in figure 2-58. Make a template from the "lower elements" portion of the drawing from figure 2-3 and use this to position and draw the curves. The curve "A" at the bottom defines the separation between the main body of the cartouche and the rope element on which it sits. The curve "B" at the right defines the connection between the lower right element and the outside edge. Note the smooth flow of these curves.

Set in along the bottom curve as shown in figure 2-59 and remove the material shown to a depth of about 1⁄8". Use a small, flat chisel or a small, shallow gouge to remove the waste.

Next set in along the curve at the right as shown in figure 2-60 and remove the material on the outside. There is a ribbon detail in this outside section that is significantly below the front, so the section needs to be lowered appropriately. Repeat until it looks like figure 2-61. Note that the depth is greater toward the bottom. The depth here is about 5⁄8". Also note that the material gets pretty thin where it meets the outside edge. Keep about 1⁄8" thickness here for structural integrity.

Use the "lower elements" template again to draw the lines as shown in figure 2-62. Note how the line at point "A" flows into the ridge surrounding the bottom of the scroll. Set in along the undulating line and bevel the background into this line. Figure 2-63 shows the result. Use #7 6 mm and 10 mm gouges to match the curves and small, shallow gouges to lower the background. Note how the ridge line around the scroll flows into this one.

Figure 2-57. The rabbet isolates the rope on the bottom. Also isolate it on top. Then round over the surface of the rope with a #7 10 mm gouge oriented with the bevel up.

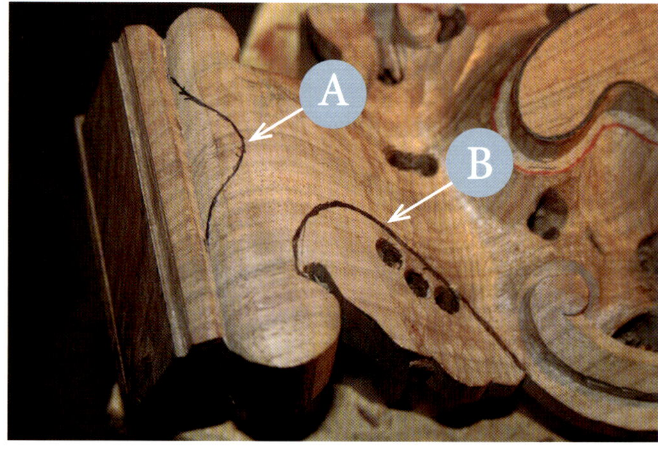

Figure 2-58. Connect the bottom scrolls with curve "A." Curve "B" connects the right scroll with the right side of the cartouche and defines the ribbon detail tucked into the bottom scroll.

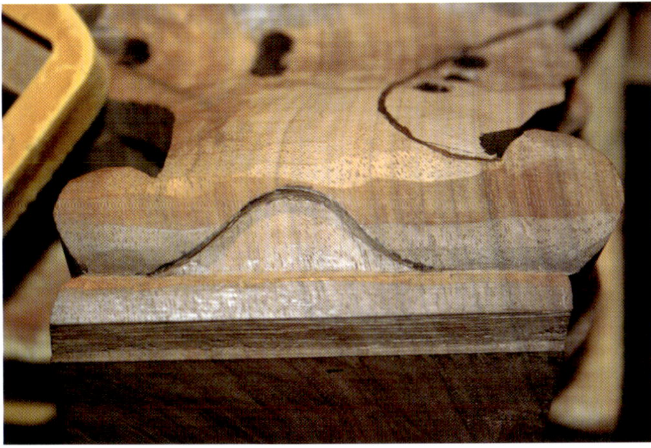

Figure 2-59. Lower the background in the area between the two bottom scrolls and the rope.

Figure 2-60. Set in along the line as shown and remove material on the outside.

Figure 2-61. Continue to lower the ribbon detail section. Note how the thickness varies from near the scroll at the bottom and farther up toward the center.

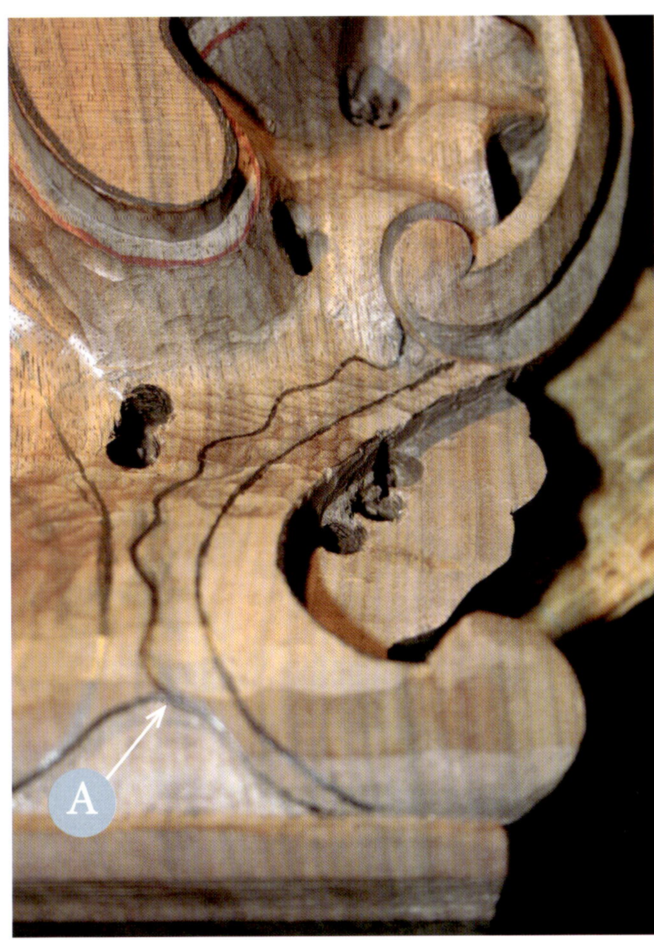

Figure 2-62. This undulating line defines another ribbon detail.

Figure 2-63. Raise this ribbon by setting in along the line and lowering the background into it.

Next sketch in the leaves as shown in figure 2-64. Because of the surface shape, tight fit, and the topographical constraints of the leaves, draw these lines freehand. Note that the leaf labeled "A" is just below one hole. The leaf labeled "B" flows around the lower piercing of the C-scroll and bottoms out at the base of the peanut butte.

Separate the leaf from the peanut butte as shown in figure 2-65. Now use a V-tool to separate the leaves in the cluster as shown in figure 2-66. Open up the button as shown in figure 2-67 by setting in around the button and then beveling into it with a #7 10 mm gouge.

Figure 2-68 shows this section complete. Use this figure to see how the various elements work together and refine the leaf cluster appropriately. The separation line is low and the surfaces on either side of the line are rounded with a convex curvature down to the bottom of the line. The leaf labeled "A" is high on the outside edge and falls off toward the shelf below the C-scroll. The middle section of the leaf labeled "B" is high in the middle and rounded over on both sides left and right. The leaf labeled "C" falls off at least ¼" down to the background at the bottom of the peanut butte. Finally, enlarge and shape the piercing "D" as shown.

Figure 2-64. Draw a leaf cluster that connects the scroll at the bottom, falls off the side, and tucks into and around the central C-scroll.

Figure 2-65. Separate the top of the leaf from the base of the peanut butte.

Figure 2-66. Separate the leaves in the cluster with a V-tool.

Figure 2-67. Open the button at the bottom. Set in around the curve of the button and cut into it with a #7 10 mm gouge.

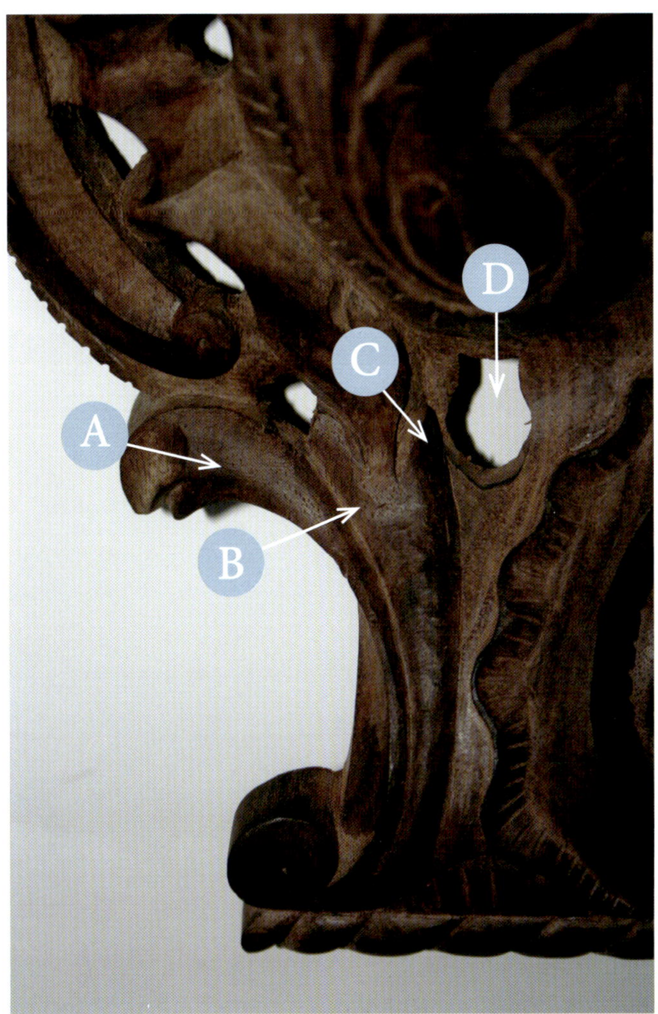

Figure 2-68. A view of this completed section. Use this as a guide for shaping the individual elements.

Return to the lower right side. Use a V-tool to separate the elements as shown in figure 2-69. Note how the V-cut feathers out at the scroll.

Draw the lines as shown in figure 2-70. Set in around the button and use a #7 10 mm gouge to remove the corner into the button as shown in figure 2-71. Note how the surface formed by removing the corner flattens out and blends into the ledge on the outside of the central C-scroll.

Referring to the same figure, deepen the separation line and round the surface to the right of the line as shown and bevel the surface to the left. Repeat these steps until the separation line is about 3⁄16" deep.

Use a #9 10 mm gouge to form the troughs shown in figure 2-72. This element is an undulating ribbon with alternating hills and valleys along its entire line. These trough cuts are the start of the valleys. The sections between the valleys will become the hills. Round over the edges formed by the gouge cuts until the surface looks like that in figure 2-73. I use a small, flat chisel to round the edges and a rounded scraper to remove the facets and blend the surfaces.

Draw the lines as shown in figure 2-74. Fit the curves to match the holes and outside contour. Figure 2-75 shows the completed element. To complete this element, first carve to both the inside and outside curves as shown in figure 2-76. These don't have to be perfect at this point but good enough to have the curves and cusps defined. Set in along the middle curve and bevel into the stop cut as shown in figure 2-77. A #7 10 mm gouge should work well for this. Note that the beveled surfaces are concave except for the part labeled "A", which is convex.

Figure 2-69. Separate the scroll from the ribbon next to it. Use a V-tool to cut along the boundary line.

Figure 2-70. Draw lines that will open the button.

Figure 2-71. Set in around the button and cut into it with a #7 10 mm gouge. This is the same operation as has been done on all the other similar elements.

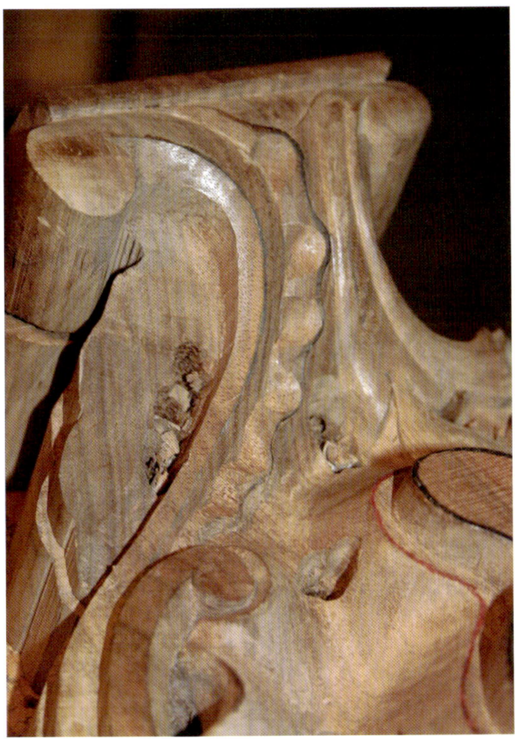

Figure 2-72. Once the separation between the scroll and the ribbon is sufficiently deep and the ribbon surface is beveled into the base of the boundary, use a #9 10 mm gouge to cut the troughs of the ribbon.

Figure 2-73. Round the edges of the gouge cuts to form convex surfaces between adjacent troughs. The final surface should be smooth and continuously up and down.

Figure 2-74. On the right side, draw the lines that define the ribbon detail.

Figure 2-75. The completed ribbon detail. Use this as a guide.

The inner portion is a repeat of the outer one. Referring to the inner part now, use a #7 10 mm gouge to scoop from the middle curve toward the inside edge, keeping the middle curve high. As before, all of the surfaces are concave except the bottom half of the bottom section, which is convex. When access gets tight near the wall, use a small skew chisel. I use a #1 3 mm double bevel chisel. This tool can get into very tight spaces and can be used for both left and right orientations because it is beveled on both sides.

Next add a similar detail to the upper right section just below the plume. Draw in the curves as shown in figure 2-78. Create a relatively flat ledge at the base of the peanut butte before placing this element. The thickness of the remaining ledge should be no more than ⅜". It should also blend into the ledge on the outside of the C-scroll. Figure 2-78 shows how the ledge flows into the outside of the C-scroll and blends into the base of the peanut butte as it terminates into the plume.

Use some narrow #9 gouges to cut the semi-circular edge profile. This is also shown in figure 2-78. Next set in along the curved portions with a #7 6 mm gouge. Bevel into these stop cuts from behind and blend the surface into the butte to raise the element. Finally, use a #9 gouge of appropriate width to scoop the individual sections. Try to get crisp cusp lines that nicely separate the sections.

Return to the left side and work on the leaves above the scroll. Note that the section above the scroll is lower than the scroll by about ⅛". Draw the lines as shown in figure 2-79. Note that the line labeled "A" approximately splits the distance moving into the plume. This line is going to be a ridge. Set in as shown in figure 2-80 and bevel into the bottom of the stop cut. The bevel starts from the ridge line and is a sloped surface into the leaf. The effect is that the leaf is sitting on an angled surface.

As the leaf is being raised above the angled surface on one side of the ridge line, angle and blend the surface on the other side down into the base of the butte and plume. Figure 2-81 shows progress at this stage. Continue working this area until it looks like figure 2-82. Separate the two leaves by setting in along the line between them and round down from leaf "A" and bevel from leaf "B." Note that the leaf "A" is rounded on both sides as well as at the edge. Leaf "B" is separated in two sections by a ridge. Use a #9 10 mm gouge to scoop concave surfaces on either side of the ridge. Leaf "B" is rounded to a convex surface at its tip. Figure 2-83 shows this section complete.

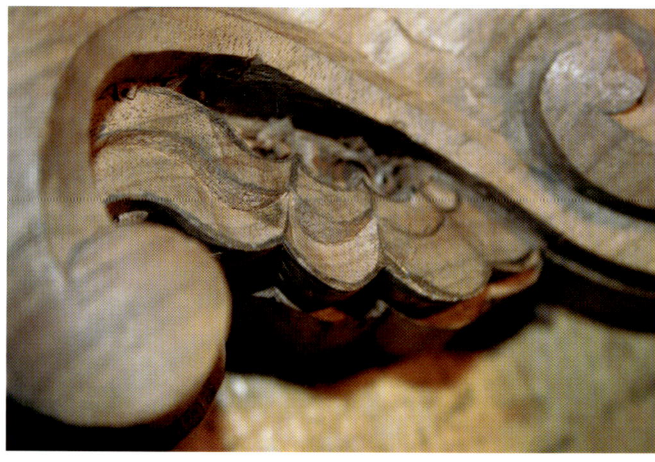

Figure 2-76. Set in along the centerline and cut into it from the outside. Note that each segment is separate and high at the boundaries between them.

Figure 2-77. Most of the surfaces in this area are concave. However, the one labeled "A" is convex. This forms an S-shaped surface.

Figure 2-78. There is a small ribbon detail just between the plume and the central C-scroll on the right side. Draw this detail to accommodate the outside profile. The outside profile may have to be modified and refined. Also this detail requires a more or less locally flat surface, so shave off the wall of the butte and sufficiently flatten the transition into the base.

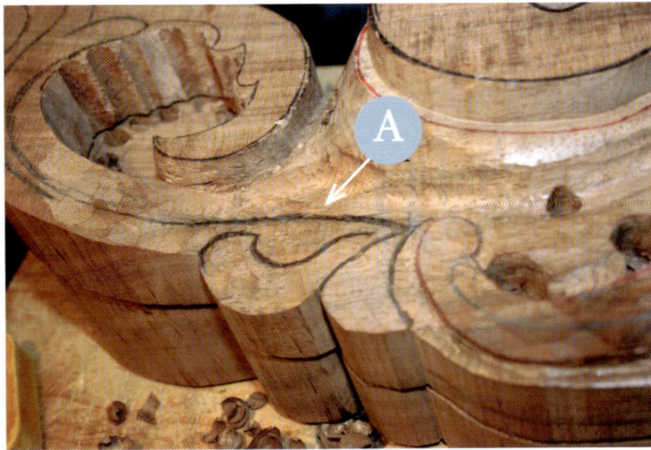

Figure 2-79. The line "A" will become a ridge that divides the plume into two surfaces and blends into the leaf cluster above the C-scroll.

Figure 2-81. From the same ridge line, slant the surface on the other side down into the base of the plume and butte.

Figure 2-80. Raise the leaves and bevel into the stop cuts, forming a slanted surface that is to the outside of the ridge dividing line.

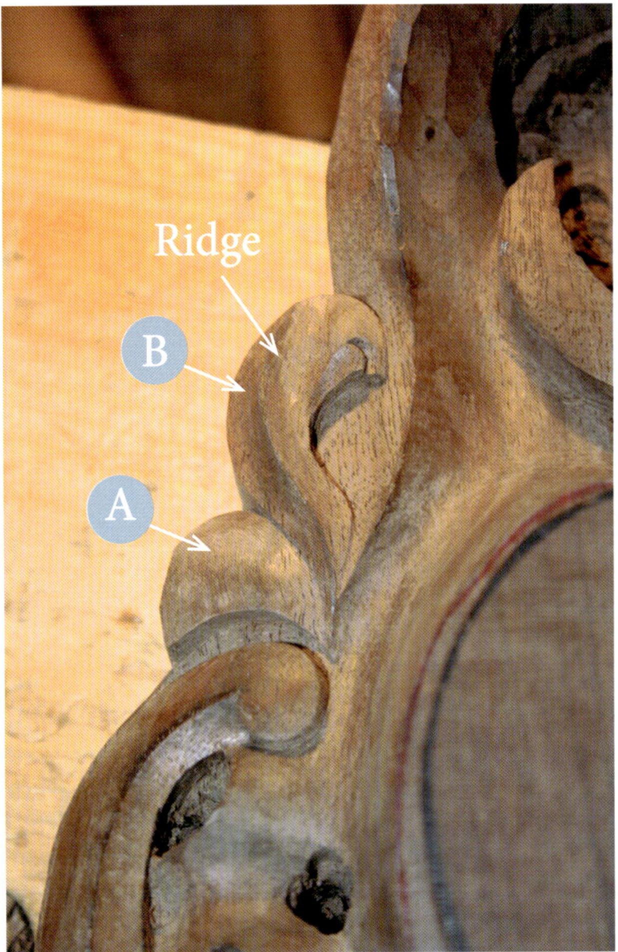

Figure 2-82. The completed leaf cluster.
Use this as a guide for how the elements fit together.

Next work on the plume section. Think of the plume as having two parts—an upper one that is the cluster of leaves at the top and flowing down to the left, and the lower part, which forms the bottom of the opening. The bottom section is lower in height than the upper. The next step is to lower the bottom section. Draw in the leaves as shown in figure 2-84. Set in along the lines labeled "A" and bevel into the stop cuts as shown in figure 2-85. Repeat until the remaining thickness is about ½". Lower the top surface of the lower plume into the bottom of the stop cut so that the thickness is about ½" the entire length. The goal is to have a more or less flat surface with no bumps that is well below the height of the upper plume.

Now rough out the upper section. Use a #49 rasp to round over the upper edge of the upper section as shown in figure 2-86. Figure 2-87 shows the result from the side. Note that the high point is the ridge line. When forming this surface, extend the rounding into the top leaf tip. Remove as much of the tip as necessary so that the surface flows smoothly into and off the tip.

There are three separate leaves in the top cluster; start to separate them next. Draw a curve as shown in figure 2-88 that defines the bottom leaf of the cluster. Note how the curve flows from the vertex of the bottom two leaves on the outside. This is important to getting a realistic look. If these lines do not flow together, your eye will immediately see that something is wrong.

Use a V-tool to carve along this curve as shown in figure 2-89. Note how the cut flows off the end of the blank at the leaf tip and how it feathers to nothing at the other end. Round the edge as shown in figure 2-90.

Figure 2-83. The leaf cluster from a different angle. Separate the two leaves first and then shape and detail each one individually.

Figure 2-84. These leaf tips will separate the top portion from the bottom.

Figure 2-85. Set in along the leaf tip lines and bevel into them from below. This will raise the upper section from the lower one.

Figure 2-87. This angle shows how the surface falls off from the ridge line.

Figure 2-86. The contour of the upper section is such that it falls back from the dividing ridge line. Use a rasp to remove the forward edge.

Figure 2-88. Draw a line that defines the lower leaf in the cluster.

Figure 2-89. Carve along this line with a V-tool. This cut feathers to nothing on the left side and flows off the blank between the leaf tips at the top.

Next draw the curve that is also shown in figure 2-90. This defines the separation between the top and middle leaves. Again note where the curve begins at the leaf tips and how if flows almost parallel to the bottom leaf. The curve converges a little at the other end. Note that the remaining surface is almost split in two by the curve.

Now carve along this curve with the V-tool as done for the bottom leaf and shown in figure 2-91. Round the edge into the bottom of the V-cut.

The middle leaf has two surfaces from this view. Draw a curve as shown in figure 2-92. Note that the curve starts from the center tip point and blends into the ridge as shown. The two surfaces of the middle leaf will meet at this line and slant in opposite directions from it. The top leaf also has two surfaces. Draw a curve as shown in figure 2-93. Note that this curve blends into the ridge between the top and middle leaves.

Bevel from the centerlines just drawn as shown in figure 2-94. Use a #5 8 mm gouge for the curved areas and a flat or shallow gouge for the others. Make the surfaces smooth and the lines flowing so there are no irregularities that your eye is sure to notice. The back surfaces of the top two leaves still need work, but that will come a bit later.

Draw the curves as shown in figure 2-95. These separate the lower plume into three leaves. Note how the line "A" is placed. This is going to be the bottom edge of the bottom leaf. Make sure this curve flows nicely into the outside lines of the blank on the right side. Cut down from line "A" to the background at an angle. The idea is to take little or no wood off near the background. Figure 2-96 shows early progress. Continue until there is a smooth surface down to the background.

Figure 2-96 also shows leaf "B" raised. Set in along the curve that defines leaf "B" and bevel into the cut as shown. Next set in along line "C" and bevel into this cut from leaf "B." The goal is to have a stair-step stacking of the leaves. The top surfaces of the leaves wrap around toward the outside edge on the right and taper as the edge nears. Figure 2-97 shows the idea.

Figure 2-97 also shows a few other details. First there is the tip of a fourth leaf sitting on top of leaf "3." Draw in the curve, set in along it, and bevel into the cut as before. A #7 10 mm gouge should work nicely for the curve.

Figure 2-90. Round the surface of the lower leaf into the base of the V-cut. The difference in depths here is slight, but it is enough to cast a shadow that shows the individual leaves. Draw a line that defines the next leaf of the cluster.

Figure 2-91. Use a V-tool to establish the second leaf. This is the same technique as used for the first leaf.

Figure 2-92. The second, or middle, leaf has two surfaces. Draw the line that is the boundary between the two. It starts at the point of the leaf tip and blends into the ridge of the V-cut as shown.

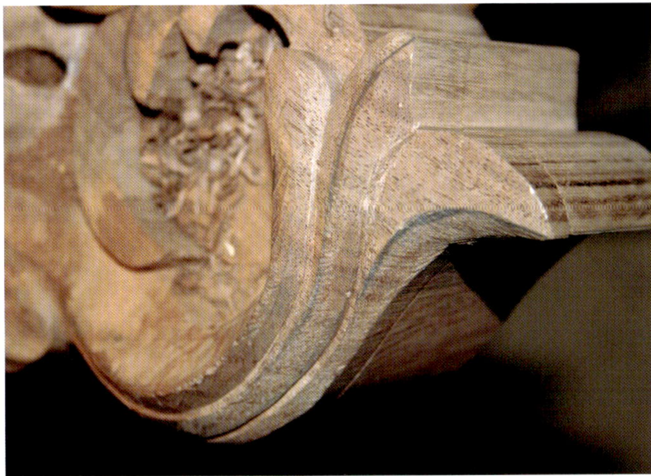

Figure 2-93. The top leaf also has two surfaces. Draw the boundary line beginning at the tip and blending into the V-cut above the first one.

Figure 2-96. Leaves "A," "B," and "C" are stacked in a stair-step configuration. Draw the defining lines for each leaf using the tips as guides.

Figure 2-94. Bevel from the centerlines just drawn into the base of the V-cuts. Deepen the V-cuts as needed.

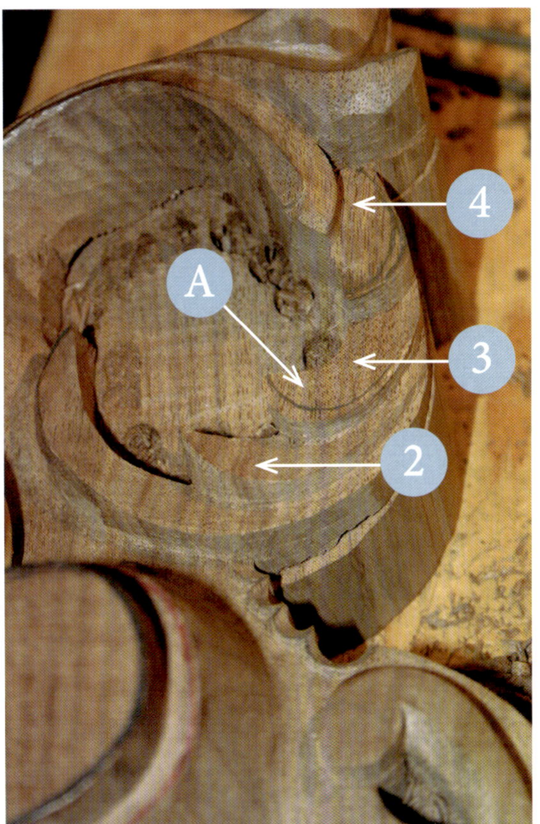

Figure 2-97. The line "A" is the ridge line for leaf #3. Angle the surface from this line down to the top of leaf #2. Also note that leaf #4 is on top of #3 and tucked into the top cluster.

Figure 2-95. The lower portion of the plume also has three leaves. This line connects the tip of the lower leaf and blends into common origin on the right side.

When leaf "3" is sufficiently lowered, about ¼", draw line "A." Angle down from this line to the leaf below as was done in the previous case. This puts the bottom edge of the leaf at an angle, which is visually more appealing. Although it is not shown, do the same treatment on leaf "2." Figure 2-98 shows this section more or less complete. Note how the fourth leaf has a rounded back side. Also note how all of the leaves converge on the outside edge. Figure 2-99 shows this from another angle.

Still referring to figure 2-98, there is a leaf detail that is commonly used in all Philadelphia foliage carving. The lines show where this detail is placed. The way to do this is to set in with a #7 4 mm gouge and take a relatively steep bevel into the cut. The opening is deepest on the outside and the two cuts meet on the inside. Figure 2-100 shows a top view of the stacked leaves.

Draw the line as shown in figure 2-101. This line is the extension of the fourth leaf just discussed. Recess the surface below this line so that none of it sticks forward of the leaf on top. This will further the illusion of one leaf on top of the other. Figure 2-102 shows the idea.

The top two leaves on the plume need some shaping on the back. First file the top back edge as shown in figure 2-103. The idea here is to have the ridge line be the only visible line as viewed from the front. If the surface behind the ridge is not beveled back, it will be visible and the overall line will be more bulky and less appealing. By beveling this surface it becomes invisible in the front view and the line looks crisper and more delicate. Taper this back surface to nothing as it wraps around the top and terminates at the leaf on the left above the C-scroll.

Figure 2-104 shows the unfinished back and edge of the top two leaves. Draw the lines as shown in figure 2-105 and use a V-tool to slightly separate the elements. Figure 2-106 shows a different view. The line on the middle leaf tip is going to become a ridge that connects the bottom, front, and back surfaces. Figure 2-107 shows this area more well defined. Four surfaces meet at a point on the end of the middle leaf tip.

Figure 2-98. Each of the bottom leaves has a ridge that defines their edge. The ridges converge on the right side as they wrap around the surface. Each ridge line is formed by an angled bottom surface and a slightly scooped top one.

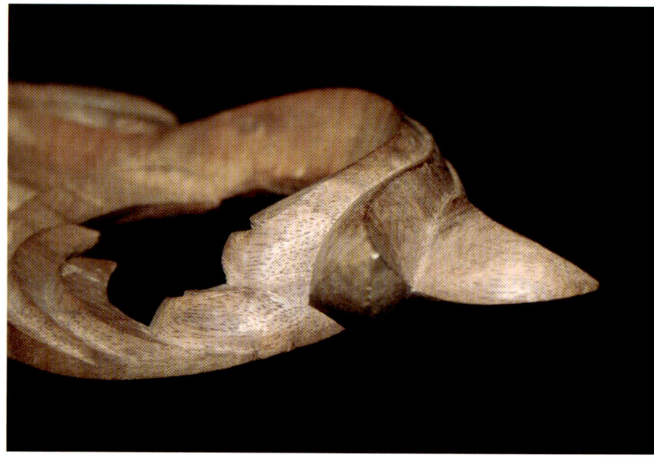

Figure 2-99. This image better shows the height variation of the bottom leaves and how they converge as they wrap around the side.

Figure 2-100. Still another view of how the leaves in the plume are stacked on top of each other and the surfaces that define them.

Figure 2-101. Leaf #4 from figure 2-97 is on the bottom of the top cluster. It extends around and underneath the others. This line defines that extension.

Figure 2-102. Use a rasp to angle the surface backward from the leaf extension line just drawn.

Figure 2-103. Shape the back side of the top leaf. The surface begins at the tip and is about half the width of the leaf. It also wraps around the entire plume and feathers to nothing on the other side.

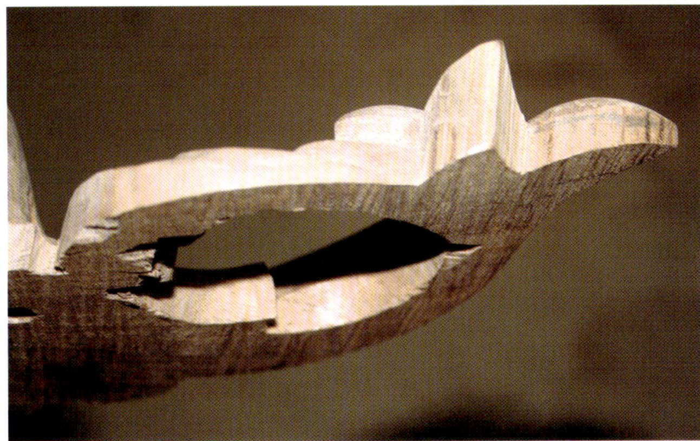

Figure 2-104. The leaves need more work on their back side.

The line in figure 2-106 becomes the ridge "A" in figure 2-107. Note how surface "1" in 2-106 needs to be refined to become surface "1" in 2-107. Note also how the corner "C" in 2-106 is removed up to the line and becomes part of surface "1" in 2-107. The ridge "B" in 2-107 does not exist in 2-106, but is drawn after the rough surface "1" in 2-106 is brought to the point "Z." Finally, round the back side of the top leaf as shown in figure 2-108. This also shows how all the surfaces relate to each other.

Now it's time to work on the peanut. The peanut and the butte on which it sits might be a little oversized at this point. If they are, trim them now. Trim the peanut so that what is left fits the template from figure 2-3. This means cut to the inside of the layout line. When that is done, mark and trim the width of the ledge on the butte to ⅛". This means that the walls of the butte need to be trimmed and blended into the background. When this is done it should look like figure 2-109.

The entire perimeter of the peanut needs to be rounded. Use a flat chisel to remove the corner as shown in figure 2-110. In the tight curved area, use a #9 gouge. Continue rounding until the entire surface is smooth and looks like figure 2-111. It will take a while to get the surface smooth and uniform. Use scrapers, files, and sandpaper if needed to get a nice surface.

Figure 2-105. The lines define how the surfaces on the back will be established. Use a V-tool to separate the leaves along these lines.

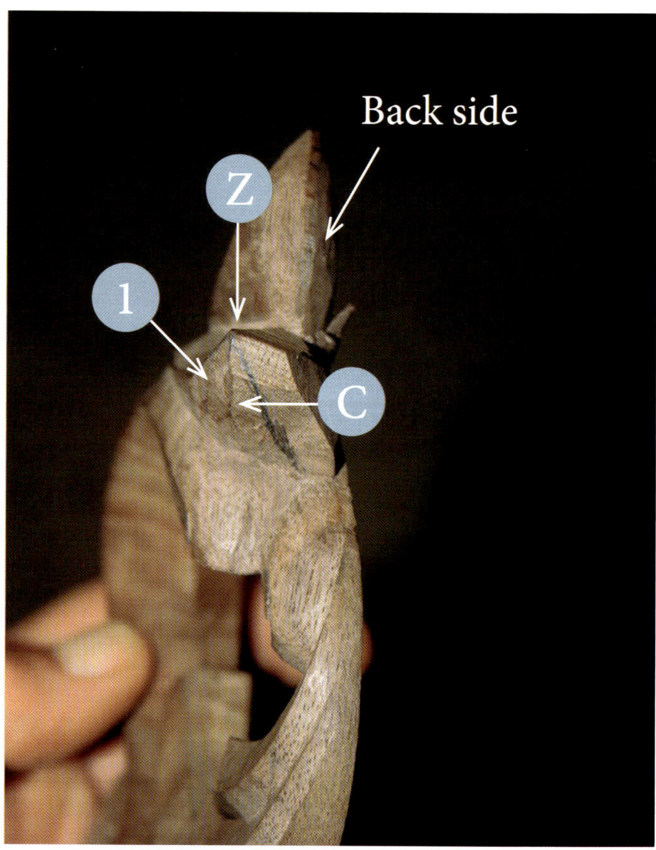

Figure 2-106. This figure and the next one are before-and-after views of this area. Study how the landmarks in 2-106 become the ridges and surfaces in 2-107. Notice also how the point "Z" evolves.

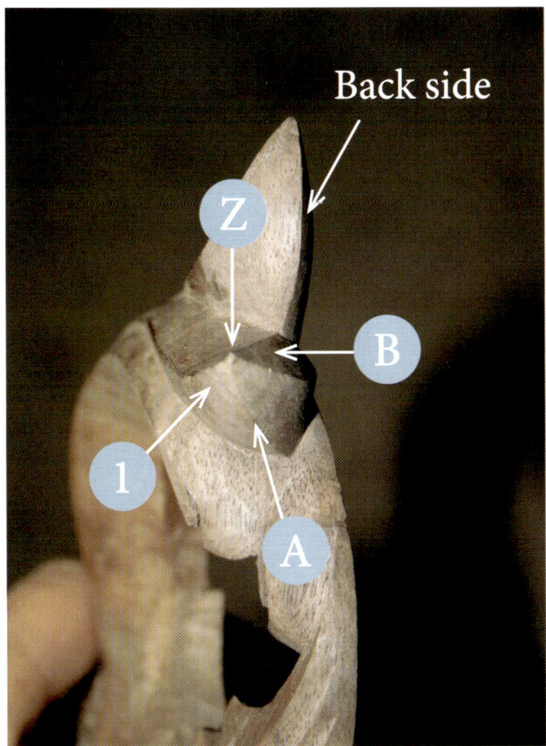

Figure 2-107.

Figure 2-109. The peanut has been reduced to fit the template and is ready to be shaped.

Figure 2-108. The back side surface of the top leaf is rounded between adjacent ridge lines.

Figure 2-110. Round the edges with a flat chisel.

Make a separate template for the leaf that is on top of the peanut and transfer it as shown in figure 2-112. Some freehand drawing is going to be needed because the template cannot lay flat on the surface. The key things to note are the location of the top flower, how the stem wraps around the bottom, and how the two leaf tips flow down the left side.

Set in along the perimeter using gouges that match the curves. Number 7s work well for the tighter curves and #2s, #3s, and #5s for the shallower ones. Bevel into the stop cuts to raise the foliage. Figure 2-113 shows some progress. Blend the background around the foliage to get a smooth surface. Figure 2-114 shows this operation almost complete.

Now detail the leaves. Draw curves as shown in figure 2-115. These lines separate the leaves. Use a V-tool to carve along the lines as shown in figure 2-116. When viewing the peanut from the front in its normal upright position, most of the leaves round from right to left. Note the details "A."

Figures 2-117 and 2-118 show the side leaves separated and detailed. Figure 2-119 shows the center leaf. Note the ridge down the center. The surface is rounded convex on the left and concave on the right. Note that there is a similar detail at the tip of the leaf as used previously. At this point the peanut is complete.

Figure 2-111. The peanut is sufficiently rounded. Strive for a smooth and uniform surface without any facets.

Figure 2-112. Draw the foliage on the peanut. Note how the leaf at the bottom wraps around.

Figure 2-113. Raise the foliage above the peanut surface. Set in along the perimeter line and cut into the stop cut.

Figure 2-114. Blend the edges from raising the foliage into the background surface.

Figure 2-115. Draw lines that define the individual leaves in the cluster.

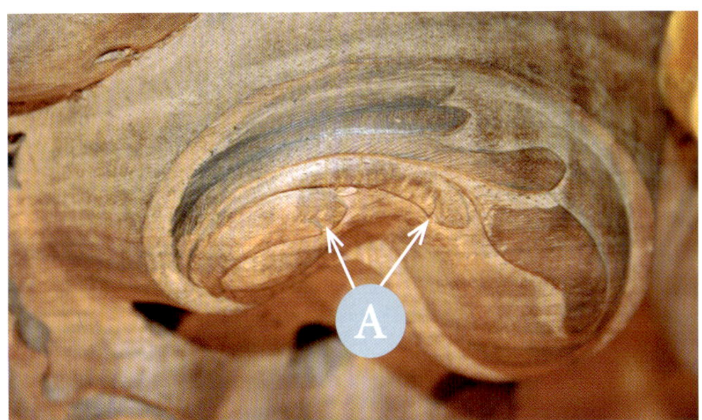

Figure 2-116. Add the typical leaf tip detail. This tucks a smaller leaf into the larger one.

Figure 2-117. Draw the separation line on the lower two leaves.

The rope element at the bottom is next. Mark divisions ½" apart as shown in figure 2-120. The goal is to partition the length into approximately equal sections. If the length isn't a multiple of ½", distribute the difference between the segments so your eye cannot tell the difference. In my case I was short an ⅛", so I made each of the end divisions 7⁄16" and the rest ½".

First draw vertical lines at the division marks as shown in figure 2-121. Then connect the bottom of one division to the top of the one adjacent as also shown in figure 2-121. Carve along the angled lines as illustrated in figure 2-122. Use a V-tool for this or set in along the line and bevel in from both sides. The latter method worked better for me in this case. Repeat these steps to widen the V-cut and curve the ends as shown in figure 2-123. Round over the edges of each section. Figure 2-124 shows the result.

The cartouche is substantially complete at this point. Figure 2-125 shows the results so far. What remains is to add accent lines on some of the elements and remove a lot of material from the back. The back is carved away to reduce the thickness around the piercings, which yields visually crisper lines. This also gives it a more delicate look, which is desirable.

Figure 2-118. Separate the leaves with a V-tool and scoop the centers a little.

Figure 2-119. The center leaf is complete.

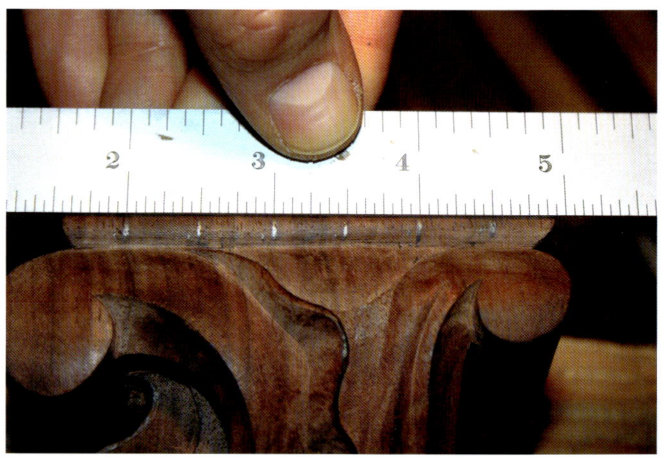

Figure 2-120. Divide the rope into ½" segments. If the length is such that not all of the segments can be ½", distribute the difference among a few so that it will not be noticeable to the eye.

Figure 2-121. Use the ½" marks as guides to draw S-shaped curves between adjacent ones.

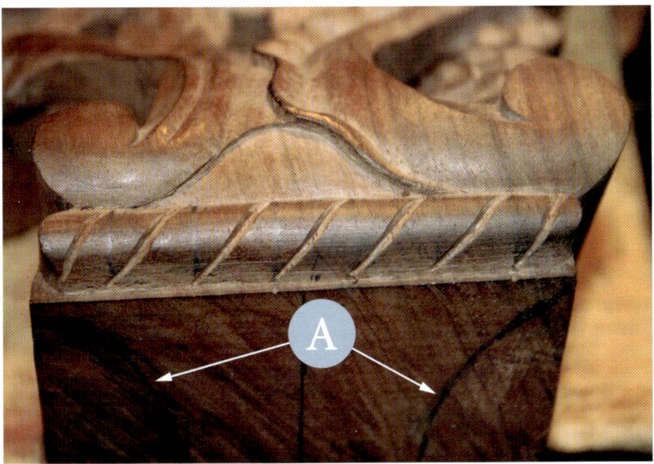

Figure 2-122. Carve a "V" along the S-curves. Set in along the line and bevel into it from each side. The lines "A" determine material to be removed later.

Figure 2-123. Progress making the V-cuts. Note the flare and its direction at the end of each curve.

Figure 2-124. Round over the edges of each section. The rope is now complete.

Figure 2-125. The cartouche is mostly done. All of the elements are defined and shaped. What remains is to lighten the back and cut accent marks on some of the elements.

PHILADELPHIA CARTOUCHE

To carve out the back, the cartouche needs to be clamped face down. To protect the carved elements, I put a towel, folded a few times, on the bench and then clamp the cartouche on top of that. Figures 2-126, 2-127, and 2-128 show the back sufficiently removed. Be aggressive when removing the back material. As long as there is structural integrity, you haven't taken off too much. The thickness around the thinner openings on mine is 3/16". When removing material from the back, carve to lines labeled "A" in figure 2-122. Leave a flat spot approximately 1½" wide to mount a supporting bracket.

The last thing to do is add accent lines to some of the carved elements. I used a #11 1 mm gouge for all of the accent marks. There are serration marks on the outside edge of the C-scrolls. Figure 2-129 shows the idea. On the right side, continue the marks all the way down to the button on the bottom. Figure 2-130 shows this. When making these cuts, be sure to use the cradle as backing support to avoid tear-out. Figure 2-130 also shows marks in the outer layer of element "A." Next add the marks on the peanut butte as shown in figure 2-131. Stop these cuts a little short of the background.

Figure 2-132 shows the finished cartouche. Now you need to build a case on which to display it.

Figure 2-126. The back has been lightened quite a bit. Note also that the corners from figure 2-122 have been carved away.

Figure 2-127. Remove sufficient material so that the edges are relatively thin. This will give a much lighter and nicer look.

Figure 2-128. The goal is to remove as much wood as possible without impacting the structural integrity of the cartouche. The shape of the back will somewhat follow that of the front.

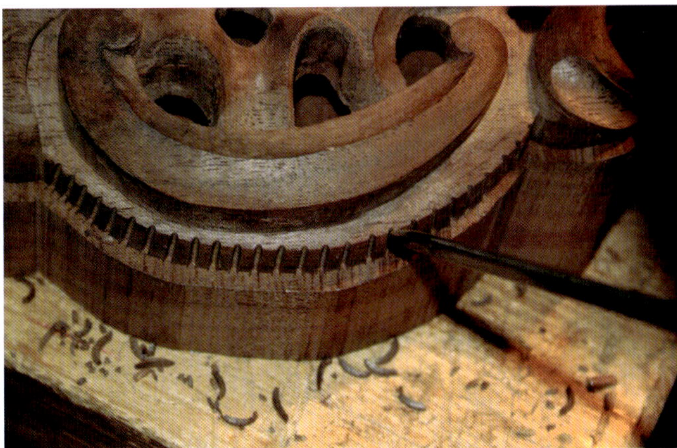

Figure 2-129. Use a #11 1 mm gouge to serrate the edges surrounding the central C-scrolls. Use the cradle as backing to avoid tear-out on the back side.

Figure 2-130. Use a #11 1 mm gouge to cut the radial lines as shown. Note also how the serration cuts continue all the way to the button at the bottom.

Figure 2-131. Cut the lines as shown on the sides of the peanut butte with a #11 1 mm gouge. Note how they form a serrated perimeter on the ledge. They also feather out just before the butte transitions to the background.

Figure 2-132. The cartouche is complete and ready to adorn the top of a deserving case piece.

PHILADELPHIA APPLIED PIERCED SHELL MEDALLION

A shell medallion, like the one described in this chapter, is a centered element usually flanked by symmetric foliage. This element would be applied to a flat surface like a table side or the scroll board on a high chest or tall case clock. The piercings add visual drama and lightness, which enhance the element and draw one's eye. Since this element is more sophisticated both stylistically and technically, it would have been found on only the finest case work.

The example that I am going to describe in this chapter is sized for a Philadelphia tall case clock. The model for this medallion is on a clock featured in the book *Timeless—Masterpiece American Brass Dial Clocks* by Frank Hohmann, pages 270–271. As of this writing there are pictures available on the web at *http://www.winterthur.org/hohmann/show_group.htm?group=79&img=79.9.jpg*. Although it is relatively small, there is much detail and refinement that will challenge your skill, provide a great sense of satisfaction, and enhance whatever piece it adorns.

One of the most difficult things to visualize and understand is the shape, contour, and flow of the background on which all of the detail will reside. When studying pictures of the finished element, try to erase the detail with your mind and eye and visualize the surface that is left. Look for what is high and low. How do the undulating surfaces flow? How do adjacent elements come together and interact? How do lines flow together and delineate surfaces? Reading photographs is a learned skill that takes time to develop. However, as you critically study photographs and carved objects, your eye will develop so that you will increasingly be able to extract more information from pictures. This is one big step to becoming more independent as a furniture maker, and critical for carving embellishments.

This medallion is part of a three-piece carved ensemble that will be attached to the scroll board of a clock. Figure 3-1 shows a scaled down version of how the elements fit together. The next chapter will describe the applied carved foliage.

To start the medallion, make a template from the line drawing in figure 3-2. Cut out the template using the same carving tools that you will use to carve the medallion. Small to medium sweep #2s, #3s and #5s are most useful with a #7 4 mm and 6 mm for the tighter curves. This technique yields nice, clean lines and good detail in the smaller areas. Figure 3-3 shows the template.

PIERCED MEDALLION CARVING DRAWING

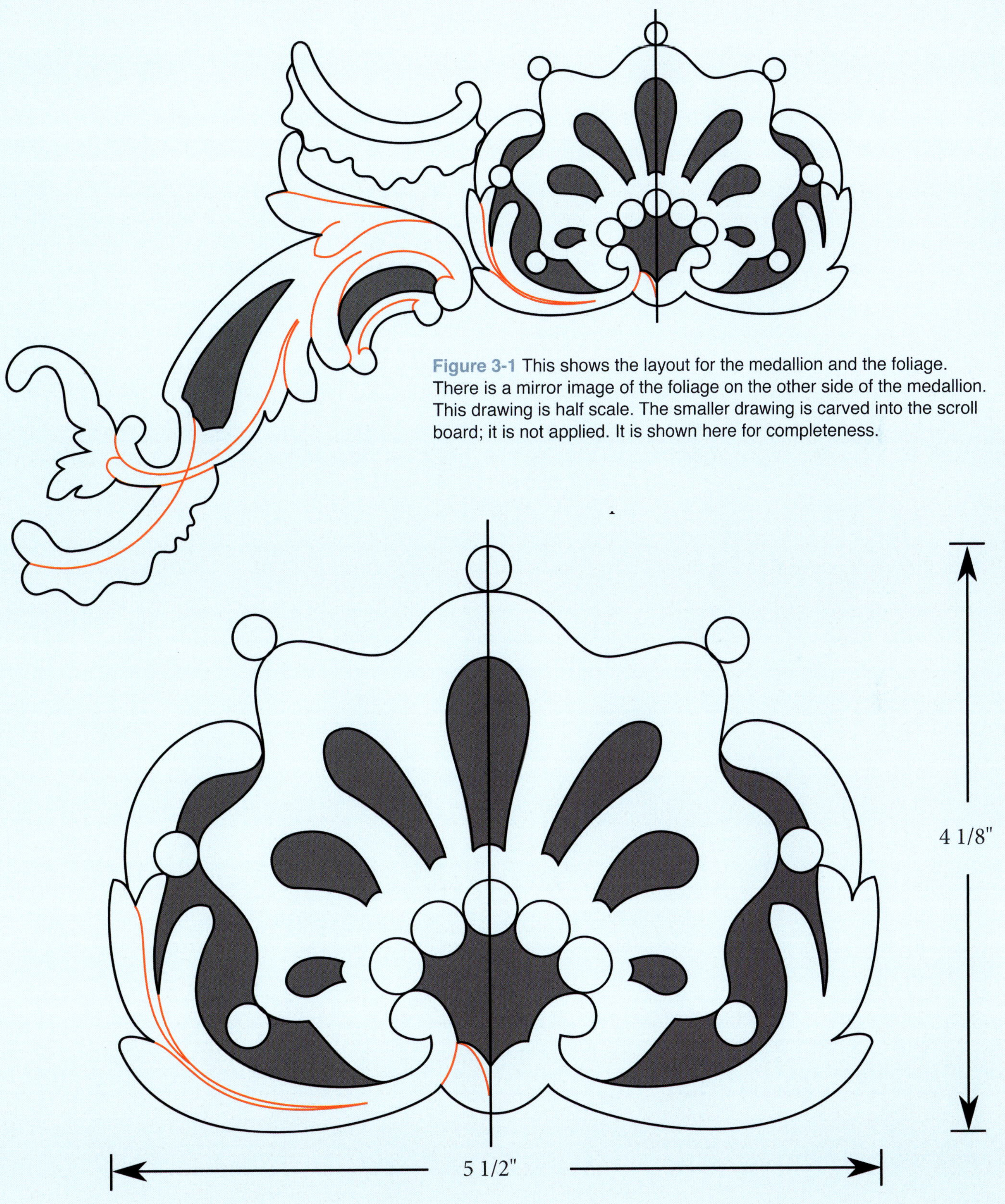

Figure 3-1 This shows the layout for the medallion and the foliage. There is a mirror image of the foliage on the other side of the medallion. This drawing is half scale. The smaller drawing is carved into the scroll board; it is not applied. It is shown here for completeness.

Figures 3-2 This is a full-scale drawing of the medallion. The gray areas are cut out.

PIERCED SHELL MEDALLION

Next trace the template on a ⅜"-thick piece of stock. Anything between ¼" and ⅜" is fine. Three-eighths of an inch is on the thick side and I will have to remove more wood as I carve, but it will give me a little more height for the high spots. A ¼"-thick piece would be completely acceptable and I probably would not have to remove as much along the way. The point here is that there is a range of acceptability and not one absolute right size. Figure 3-4 shows the template traced on the stock.

Now drill a small hole in each of the areas that are an interior cut. These are needed so that the saw blade can be inserted, since there is no access from the outside. A 3⁄16" hole is adequate for a scroll saw blade. Match the hole size to the blade you will use and the size of the space to be cut. Figure 3-5 shows the holes drilled. I used a scroll saw for both the interior and exterior cuts, but a band saw for the exterior ones and a fret saw or saber saw for the interior ones would also work. My experience is that a scroll saw is easier and does a much better job, so that would be my tool of choice. Make the interior cuts first because the blank is stronger and less likely to break. Figure 3-6 shows the interior cuts and figure 3-7 shows the blank cut out and ready for carving.

A few observations are needed before starting to carve. First, the outer tips of the convex lobes are high and their tails near the center are lower. Second, the troughs of the concave lobes are low and the surfaces of adjacent convex ones flow together in an undulating, rolling hill effect. Third, the central ring of beads are high, as are the terminating disks on the C-scrolls. Figure 3-7 also identifies these areas. Keep these thoughts in mind while establishing the surface and shape. Use a couple of pinch lamps to secure the carving blank to a supporting table. Figure 3-8 shows my setup.

Start the carving by isolating the lower ring of beads and C-scrolls. Use 5 mm and 8 mm #3s and #5s for most of this. The first cuts should be straight into the blank along the lines of separation. Then bevel into these cuts from one or both sides depending on the circumstance. Figure 3-9 shows the technique and figure 3-10 shows the beads separated.

In a similar manner, separate the shell from the elements that surround it. Figure 3-11 shows this step.

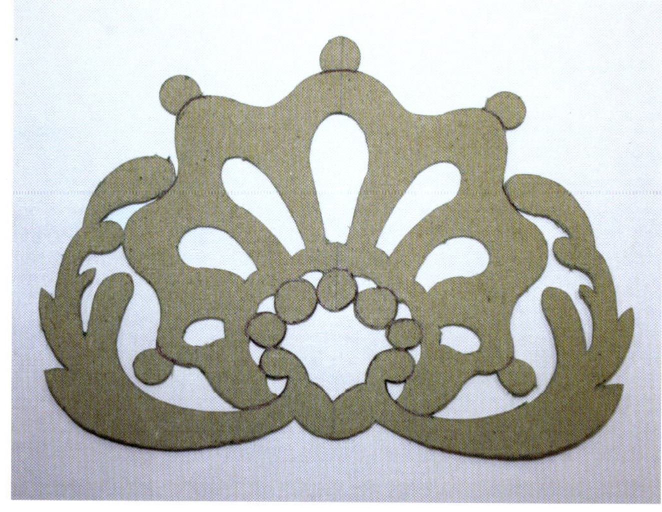

Figure 3-3. Use appropriately sized carving tools to cut out the template.

Figure 3-4. Transfer the template to the blank. Note the grain direction.

Figure 3-5. Drill access holes for the scroll saw blade.

Figure 3-6. Make the interior cuts first using a scroll saw.

Figure 3-7. Make the exterior cuts with a band or scroll saw.

Figure 3-8. Pinch clamps sufficiently hold the blank and are easy to maneuver.

Figure 3-9. Separate the central ring of beads first.

Figure 3-10. Raise the ring by lowering the background around it.

Figure 3-11. Separate the beads on the outside of the shell.

PIERCED SHELL MEDALLION

There is a downhill flow from the outer perimeter of the shell to the central ring of beads. Keeping the outer edge high, use a #3 12 mm gouge to gently slope the surface from the shell perimeter down to the bottom of the stop cuts that define the beads. The difference in height at the beads should be 1⁄16" to ⅛". Remove material near the center first and move out radially until the edges are reached. Figures 3-12 and 3-13 show the result from two angles.

Next deepen the area nearest the central beads about another ⅛" and bevel into this depth from a point about ¼" back along the entire ring. Use the same techniques as before; that is, iteratively set in along the line and bevel into the newly deepened cut. This will create a slight dropoff down into the beads and C-scroll. I used a #7 6 mm gouge to bevel close to the line and I removed the resulting facets with a #3 5 mm gouge. A small, flat chisel would also work for removing the facets. Figure 3-14 shows the result.

The next step is to shape the convex and concave lobes of the shell. The strategy is to carve a trough along the centerline of the concave lobes and round over the edges, leaving the centerline of the convex lobes untouched. To this end, sketch centerlines on all of the lobes as shown in figure 3-15. Note that the centerlines for the convex lobes are more or less through the center of the openings. Note also that all of the centerlines except the middle one are curved as they flow from the tip to the central area. Use your eye to sight these lines. In addition, put a mark ⅛" up from the bottom on the outer edge at the centerline of the concave lobes. This is the deepest portion of the concave lobe trough. Figure 3-17 shows one of these marks.

Start near the tip of one of the concave lobes with a #9 7 mm gouge and carve a shallow trough along the centerline. Figure 3-16 shows the technique. Be mindful of the grain and change directions as needed. Deepen the initial trough with the #9 7 mm gouge and expand the width of the cut near the outer edge. As the trough widens at the perimeter use wider #9s to blend the surfaces. This will yield a pleasing up and down contour. I use 10 mm and 13 mm widths for these operations. Figure 3-17 shows intermediate progress.

After a couple of iterations with the #9s, use a ½" flat chisel to round over the ridges formed by the gouge cuts. Figure 3-18 shows the technique and result. Repeat the trough cuts with the #9s and rounding the edges until the bottom of the trough hits its deepest point and the concave and convex surfaces blend smoothly. Keep in mind that the goal is to form a smooth, continuous, undulating up-and-down surface. Figure 3-19 shows the desired result.

Figure 3-12. Carve a gentle ramp from the outside perimeter down to the raised ring of beads.

Figure 3-13. The ramp as seen from a different angle.

Figure 3-14. Deepen the area next to the ring.

Figure 3-15. Draw centerlines for each of the lobes.

Figure 3-16. Use a #9 10 mm gouge to carve a trough near the edge of one of the concave lobes.

Figure 3-17. Taper the trough as it flows down toward the ring of beads.

Figure 3-18. Use a flat chisel to round over the edges of the convex lobes.

Figure 3-19. Use scrapers, files, and sandpaper to connect the concave and convex lobes in a smooth, undulating surface.

Note that the concave lobes that empty into the tip of the foliage are a little harder to access because the tip of the leaf is proud (higher) of the trough. A technique that might be helpful here is to roll the #9 gouge to better access the tight fit near the leaf tip. Start the roll by placing one corner of the gouge on the convex lobe as shown in figure 3-20. As the cut proceeds down the valley of the concave lobe, rotate the gouge clockwise until it sits in the bottom of the trough. Figure 3-21 shows the terminating position of the gouge after the roll.

There are still a few facets that need to be removed. I use a variety of tools for this cleanup, including radial scrapers, fine cut riffler files, and sandpaper, depending on the shape, grain, and access. Figure 3-22 shows one of the radial scrapers. This is also a good time to reshape the little dome protrusions at the bottom of the convex lobe openings. These are small enough that they may not come out perfect right off the scroll saw. Use a #7 4 mm or #7 3 mm gouge to reshape any that need it.

Now work on one of the leaf clusters. Begin by drawing the line shown in figure 3-23. Remove the material to the inside of this line with a #5 8 mm gouge for the flatter areas and a #7 6 mm gouge for the tighter curve. Figure 3-24 shows the result.

The entire leaf cluster that wraps around the side is sloped down toward the outside. To get the proper surface, round over the corner as shown in figure 3-25. Use a flat chisel for this operation.

Draw in the bead as shown in figure 3-26. Set in around the bead with a #7 6 mm gouge and remove the material on the outside of the bead. This will raise the bead. Figure 3-27 shows the result.

Figure 3-20. In the tight access areas, use the corner of a gouge to start the cut and roll the tool to blend into the trough.

Figure 3-21. This is the ending position of the gouge after the roll.

Figure 3-22. Clean up the facets with a rounded scraper.

Figure 3-23. This line will open up the leaf and isolate the bead.

Figure 3-24. Carve to the line and knock off the corners of the bead.

Figure 3-25. The overall shape of the leaf cluster is to fall off to the outside.

Figure 3-26. Draw in the bead.

Next draw in the individual leaves as shown in figure 3-28. Raise the two leaf tips near the bead as shown in figure 3-29. Use a V-tool to separate the other leaves as shown in figure 3-30. Continue the separation until they look as in figure 3-31. Figure 3-32 shows the same operation from another angle.

Draw the lines as shown in figure 3-33. Use a #7 4 mm gouge to separate the inner leaf tip marked "A." Then carve the surfaces on either side of the line as shown in figure 3-34. Note that the line is a ridge formed by the intersection of two surfaces. Place the ridge line so that its base falls into the point of separation of the two leaf tips.

Referring to figure 3-34 again, use a #9 10 mm gouge to scoop out the two lower leaves as shown. These don't have to be deep, just deep enough so they are not flat.

Now round over the beads. Each bead is about 1/16" lower than the lobe to which it is attached. Flatten the top to this level. Place a dot in the center and don't remove it while rounding. The dot should be the top of the hemisphere. Use a #3 5 mm gouge to round the bead blank as shown in figure 3-35. This forms a cylindrical surface. Use the same gouge to round over the corners of the cylinder to form a sphere. Use a flat riffler file to remove any remaining facets to leave a smooth, uniform surface. Figure 3-36 shows a couple of the beads complete.

Figure 3-27. Set in around the bead and separate it from the leaf.

Figure 3-28. Draw the lines for each of the leaves.

Figure 3-29. Separate the leaf tips using a #7 6 mm gouge.

Figure 3-30. Use a V-tool to cut along the leaf lines.

Figure 3-31. Extend the leaf around the corner and feather it out.

Figure 3-32. Another view of the individual leaves.

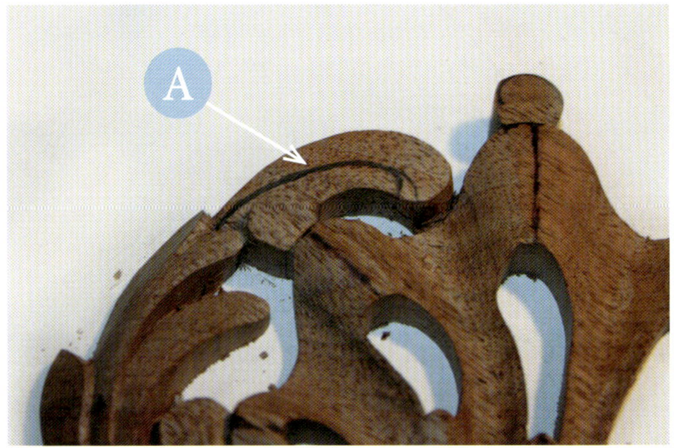

Figure 3-33. These detail lines better define the leaf.

Figure 3-34. Use a #5 gouge to define the inner leaf. Use a #7 4 mm gouge at the tip.

Figure 3-35. Round the beads. First make a curve in one direction. This forms half of a cylinder.

PIERCED SHELL MEDALLION

Work on the element at the bottom between the two leaf clusters. Figure 3-37 shows the area separated from the two clusters. Use a #9 13 mm gouge to open up the center. Then use a V-tool to separate the trough into two halves. Finally, use a #9 10 mm gouge to shape each side individually. Figure 3-38 shows the results.

Next round each bead in the ring. Separate adjacent beads using a #5 8 mm gouge. Round each bead as previously described. Clean up each bead with a riffler file and sandpaper. Figure 3-39 shows the ring of beads complete.

Figure 3-40 shows progress to this stage. If there are any machine marks or irregularities on the edges, now is a good time to clean them up. Files and scrapers work well for this. Some of the narrow interior cuts are harder to access, so small files work well. At this point the medallion is shaped and all the elements are formed. All that remains are some accent lines and punch holes. Figure 3-41 shows the lines and holes. Use a #11 2 mm gouge for the accent lines and a small nail set or awl for the holes. Be careful when making the holes. If too much force is used, the material will break.

The pierced medallion is now complete and ready to be applied to the scroll board.

Figure 3-36. Round the ends of the half cylinder to form a half sphere. Use small files to blend the facets.

Figure 3-37. Separate the lower section from the C-scrolls.

Figure 3-38. Use a #9 gouge to scoop out the center. Use a narrower #9 to define each section.

Figure 3-39. Round over each bead. Use a #7 6 mm gouge to set in around each bead. Then round the tops into the base of the separation cuts.

Figure 3-40. Smooth any remaining facets. The medallion is shaped. Only accent items remain.

Figure 3-41. The completed medallion. Use a small nail set for the holes and a #11 2 mm gouge for the accent lines.

PHILADELPHIA APPLIED PIERCED VINE

Applied carved vines are attached to a flat surface and are a high style embellishment of the finest order. They usually are used in mirror-image pairs and symmetrically flank a carved central element. Typical usage would be on a drawer front, the front skirt board on a high chest or dressing table, or the scroll board of a high chest or tall case clock.

Figure 4-1. Early Queen Anne applied vine. Note the shape is most of the detail.

On earlier pieces the vines are relatively crude, not pierced, and most of the detail is the overall shape of the element. Figure 4-1 shows an early example on the drawer front of a dressing table. As the form evolved, the shapes became more delicate, elaborate, intricate, detailed, and pierced. Figures 4-2 and 4-3 show two typical examples of a later and much richer version.

The example described in this chapter is designed for a tall case clock and is the companion of the central medallion described in chapter 3. Although it is smaller than the ones on the high chest in figures 4-2 and 4-3, it is equal in style, design, detail, and skill level required. By understanding, studying, and practicing this example, you will significantly increase your skill level and confidence. The model for this design is featured in the book *Timeless—Masterpiece American Brass Dial Clocks* by Frank Hohmann, pages 270–271. Figure 4-4 shows my version of this element.

Figure 4-2. Later Chippendale applied vine. The leaves and flowers are more realistic than the earlier form.

Figure 4-3. An applied vine on the scroll board of a Chippendale high chest.

Figure 4-4. My completed version of this chapter's project.

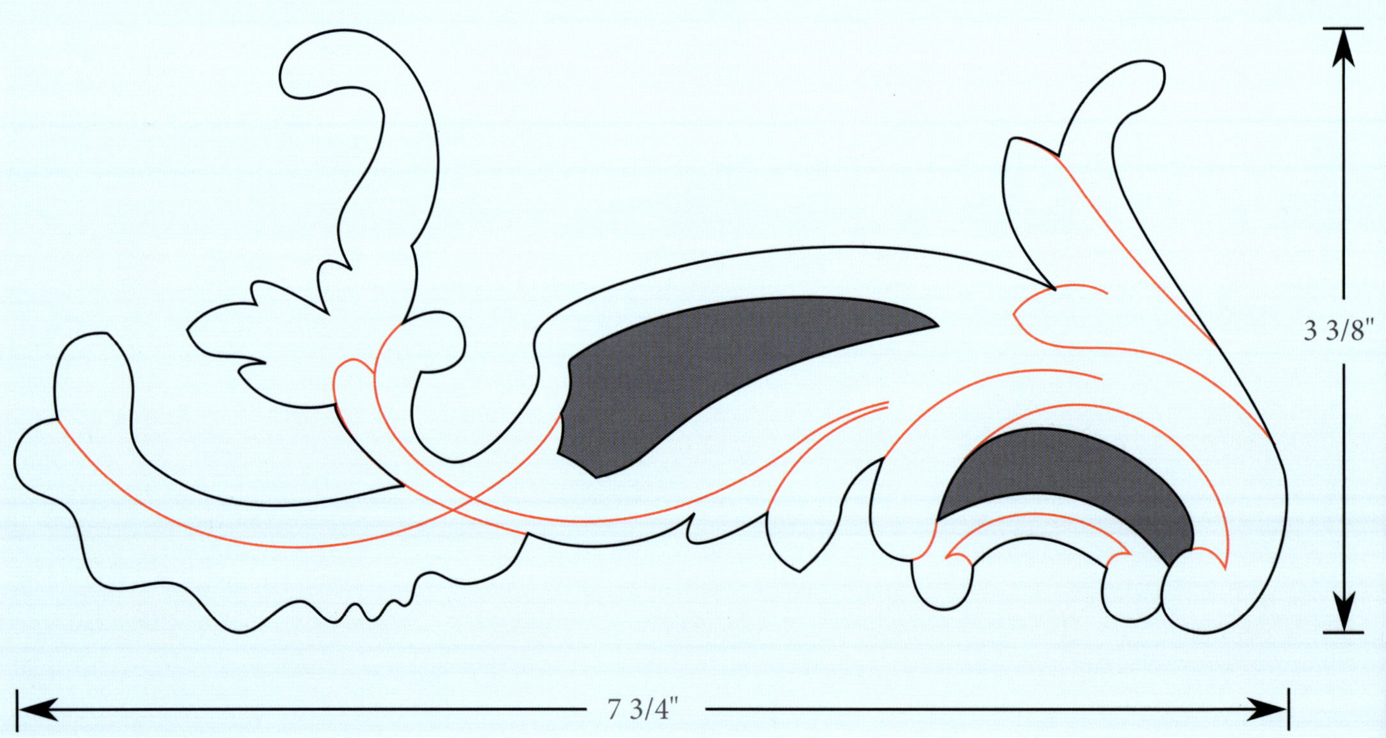

Figure 4-5. This is a full-scale drawing of the applied vine.
The gray areas are cut out. The red lines separate and detail the elements.

APPLIED PIERCED VINE

Figure 4-6. Transfer the template to the blank and drill access holes in the interior sections. Note the long direction of the template is in line with the grain.

As usual, the first step is to make a template of the element to be carved. Transfer the drawing in figure 4-5 to a piece of template material. Next cut out the template, using appropriate carving tools. This will yield crisp, clean lines and the shapes will be better formed than with a scissors.

Next transfer the template onto a piece of ¼" stock. At this point I am mainly interested in the cutout areas and the outside perimeter. Drill a 3/16" hole in each of the cutout sections. Figure 4-6 shows the template transferred to the stock and the holes drilled. Cut out the interior sections first. If the exterior is cut first, the blank is less sturdy, and thus more susceptible to breaking when doing the interior sections. I use a scroll saw for the interior cuts. A coping saw or saber saw could also be used, but my experience is that a scroll saw works best. After the interior cuts are done, do the exterior. A band saw would work here, but I think the scroll saw is better because of the tight curves. Figure 4-7 shows the blank cut out from the stock.

Figure 4-7. Cut out the interior sections with a scroll saw and the exterior ones with either a band saw or scroll saw.

Now with the template in place over the cutout blank, draw in the detail line segments as shown in figure 4-8. I only put segments on the template, because if the detail lines were completely cut, the template would not hold together. This requires connecting the segments by hand and eye, but there are enough traced segments that this is quite easy. Figure 4-9 shows the segments connected. Study the picture of the finished element and the line drawing to get all of the detail lines. Some of the detail lines have to be drawn by hand. If you miss some of them at this point, it is not a big deal because you can add them later when that portion is carved.

Figure 4-8. Use the template to locate some of the leaf separation lines.

Use a couple of pinch lamps to secure the carving blank to a supporting table. There is no one correct way to start the carving, but pay attention to the various levels and separate the larger elements before considering the detail. Try to visualize the shape of the surface without the detail and concentrate on forming that shape. Once the shape and surface are correct, the detail is relatively easy. A major mistake people make is to put in detail too early. If the levels are not more or less correct before adding detail, there will be continuous frustration because the elements will not fit together properly.

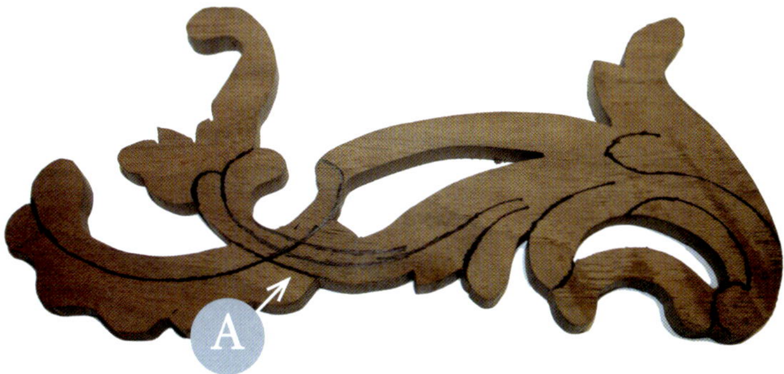

Figure 4-9. Begin by separating the upper elements along the line "A."

APPLIED PIERCED VINE

I like to start with an area where the difference in levels is a little more obvious. In this example, one such area is near line "A" in figure 4-9. In this case the ribbon flows under the sweeping frond. This positioning determines how the lines must be cut. Set in along line "A" in figure 4-9 and bevel into this cut from the ribbon side. Figure 4-10 shows the bevel cut and the separation. Next blend the valley formed by the bevel into a longer ramp toward the outside. Keep the outer tip of the ribbon section high and carve a gentle ramp into the valley. A good way to tell if the ramp is gradual enough is that you should not be able to see a dropoff when viewed from above. It should look like a smooth, straight surface. Figure 4-11 shows the desired result. Now the ribbon section toward the outside is isolated and the level is correct. Work on this area next because it does not interact with other elements, so it will be easier to visualize and shape.

There are two sub-elements to this section. One is the ribbon portion itself and the other is the leaf stem and tip. One of the detail lines drawn earlier defined the separation of these two elements. Redraw this line because much of it was removed when creating the level ramp from the last step. Set in along this line and bevel back into it. Figure 4-12 shows the results of these cuts. Use a ½" flat chisel to carve a smooth ramp from the outer edge of the ribbon into the valley just created. This is the same process that was used to isolate and shape this area in the first place. Note also that the ribbon gets lower as it approaches the tip. Connect all of these constraints with a continuous, smooth surface. Figure 4-13 shows significant progress in shaping the ribbon surface.

Next draw the line shown in figure 4-14. This line partitions the leaf lengthwise. On one side will be a convex surface and on the other will be a concave one. Use a #9 10 mm gouge to shape the concave side. Note that the concave cut goes almost to the bottom of the blank. Leave a little thickness for strength and to form a shadow. In this case 1/32" is probably more than enough. Use a ½" flat chisel to shape the convex surface on the back side of the leaf. Note that the surface falls off toward the tip of the leaf. Figure 4-15 shows both of these surfaces shaped.

Add the leaf tip detail using a #7 4 mm gouge to make a stop cut along line "A" in figure 4-16. Be careful with the pressure when making the stop cut because there is not much material here and the tip could easily snap off. With the same gouge, bevel into this cut beginning from the line "B" in figure 4-16. This bevel cut is a ramp from line "B" down into the bottom of line "A." Do this in a couple of iterations to get the final result. Figure 4-17 shows the leaf tip detail.

Figure 4-10. Set in along the line and bevel into the stop cut.

Figure 4-11. Feather the beveled ramp until there is no visible drop-off.

Figure 4-12. Redraw the leaf line. Set in along it and bevel into it from the ribbon side.

Figure 4-13. Feather the ribbon side bevel to a gentle ramp, leaving the perimeter high.

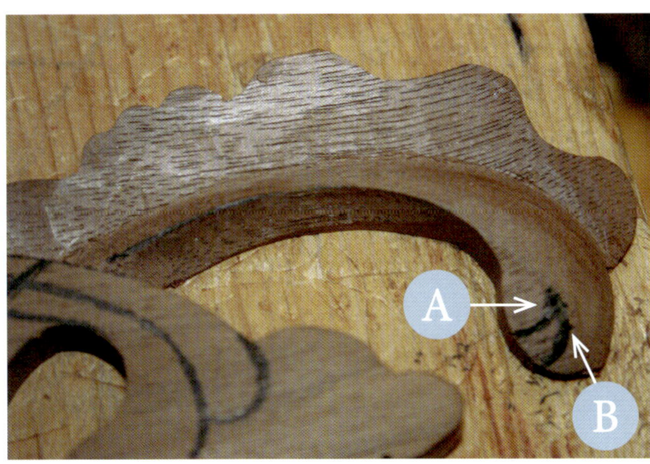

Figure 4-16. Add the leaf detail. Set in along line "A" with a #7 4 mm gouge. Bevel into cut "A" from line "B."

Figure 4-14. Draw the inside leaf line.

Figure 4-17. The leaf detail complete.

Figure 4-15. Round the leaf to a convex surface so that the inside is high.

Figure 4-18. Use a #9 7 mm gouge to cut troughs in the concave portions.

Next add the folds in the ribbon. The strategy here is to make a series of troughs and then round over the edges to form convex surfaces between two adjacent ones. There are several things going on to form the final surface. One, the perimeter is an undulating in-and-out line along the curve of the ribbon. Two, the top surface is also undulating in an up-and-down motion. These two flows come together with the convex top surface matching the inward projection on the perimeter line and the outward projection on the perimeter matching the concave surface on top. Keep this in mind while carving to make judgments about where to place elements. It is not important that each ribbon have exactly the same number of ups and downs and ins and outs, but rather that the motion and alignment of edge and surface are adequately matched. This will look good to the eye, and that is what matters.

Use #9 gouges to cut the troughs matching the width to the space available. For this one a 5 mm one will be used the most, with a 3 mm one toward the bottom. Round over the trough edges with a ¼" flat chisel or the concave side of a narrow #2. For final blending I will use radius cut scrapers or chisels as scrapers. Figure 4-18 shows intermediate progress and figure 4-19 shows the operation complete. This section of the carving is now mostly complete.

Next work on the cluster just above this one. Recall that this cluster sits on top of the ribbon. Draw the line "A" shown in figure 4-20 and set in along it. Bevel into this line in the same manner as before. This will isolate the cluster from the ribbon. Now separate the leaf labeled "B" in figure 4-20 by carving along its perimeter line with a V-tool. Note that setting in along this line and beveling into it from both sides removes equivalent material. Use the technique that works best for you. I use both of them depending on circumstances. Round over leaf "B" a little to give better access to the other portion of this cluster. Figure 4-21 shows early progress.

Note that the root of this other portion is lower and dives into a surrounding hood. Establish the hood by setting in along the perimeter line of the root using a #5 5 mm gouge and beveling a ramp into this cut. Walk the gouge around the perimeter of the root, connecting the outside edge of the blank with the separation line on the opposite side. Use the same #5 with the bevel side up to round over the tip of the root. Now with the bevel side down, cut into the root from the opposite side. This will open up the root and define the hood. Figure 4-22 shows some results.

Next shape the area from the hood to the tip of the blank. Note that the hood is high at the top of the root and falls off left and right. It also falls off in the direction

Figure 4-19. Use a flat chisel to rough the convex portions. Use files and rounded scrapers to remove the facets and smooth the surface.

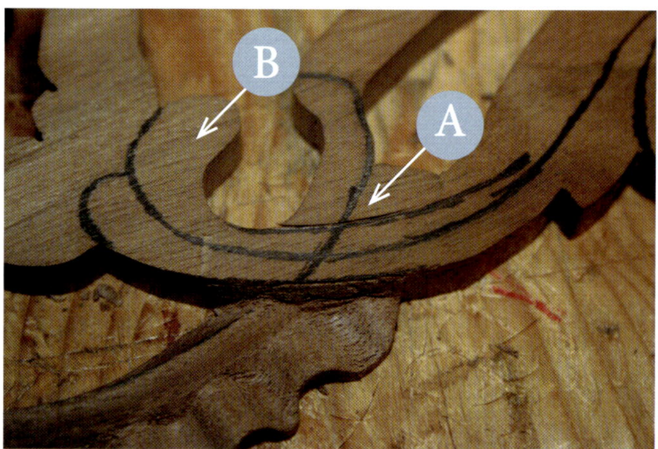

Figure 4-20. The section above line "A" is low and the inside line of leaf "B" will be low.

Figure 4-21. Set in along "A" and bevel into it from above. Set in along "B," bevel into it, and round the leaf.

Figure 4-22. Lower the other leaf and separate it from the cluster farther out.

Figure 4-23. Note that the hood is high where it surrounds the leaf that settles into it.

Figure 4-24. Lower the C-scroll.

Figure 4-25. Round over the corner.

Figure 4-26. Use a V-tool to separate the upper and lower sections.

Figure 4-27. Round the upper corner of the lower section.

of the extended leaf. Think of the hood as the apex of a cone that falls off in all directions. The overall surface of this conical shape is convex. Use a ½" flat chisel to rough in the cone.

Define and separate the leaf tips using a #5 5 mm gouge. Further define each leaf with #9 gouge cuts down the axis of each leaf. These cuts are shallow and the goal is to create slight ridge lines that will separate adjacent leaves. These ridges are subtle yet definite. The shadows that the ridges and valleys create will tell the eye how each leaf is shaped. Figure 4-23 shows the result.

Continue by shaping the extending leaf. The cross section of this leaf as it starts to extend is a convex hump. Round this over on each side with a ¼" flat chisel. As this progresses along the length of the leaf, the shape is convex on one side and concave on the other. Finally, there is a tip detail similar to the previous section that is formed the same way. Figure 4-23 also shows this complete.

This one end of the blank is now mostly shaped and carved. Go to the other end and work on that. When that is done, blend the two ends by carving the area between them. Start by isolating the small C-scroll at the bottom. Note that this is lower than the surrounding element. Draw in some delineation lines, set in where needed, and lower the C-scroll with a flat chisel. Figure 4-24 shows the operation complete.

Refer to figure 4-4 and study the flow of the big leaf cluster that emanates from the button on the lower right. Visualize the surface shape without the detail. Put another way, try to visualize the envelope that would shrink wrap around the cluster. The button is high and the surface drops off to the right. This whole corner is rounded from the top all the way to the bottom of the blank. Walking along the surface up and toward the center of the blank, the slope is down toward the left-hand cutout and high near the right-hand cutout. With these ideas in mind, use a flat chisel to round over the outer corner. Figure 4-25 shows this step. Next use a V-tool to separate the sub-cluster that flows up and to the right from the one that flows down and toward cutout 1. This separation is necessary because the surfaces have different shapes going in different directions and they need to be worked on independently. Figure 4-26 shows the separation cut.

Now that the two elements are separated, refine the shape of each individually and alternately until each is sufficiently formed. Work on the one that flows down to cutout 1 first. Round the edge as shown in figure 4-27. Next separate the other side from the leaf next to it. Set in along the leaf line and bevel into the bottom of the stop cut. Repeat these steps until the lower section

Figure 4-28. The lower section blends into leaves that flow over the ribbon. Note how the center is high and the surface falls off in both directions.

Figure 4-29. Define the leaf tip.

Figure 4-30. This leaf tip sits on top. Use a #7 6 mm gouge to define its shape.

Figure 4-31. Form a gentle ramp into the base of the leaf tip.

Figure 4-32. Shape the ribbon section on the top portion of the cutout. Use a #9 5 mm gouge to place the end troughs first.

Figure 4-33. Position the high spots on the convex portions.

Figure 4-34. Use a #9 7 mm gouge to cut troughs between the convex portions.

Figure 4-35. Round the edges formed by the gouge cuts with a flat chisel.

Figure 4-36. Position the inside surface of the C-scroll with the lines shown.

is about 1/16" high. Figure 4-28 shows the result. The ridge formed in figure 4-28 flows into the stem that was carved earlier and should remain high. Isolate the leaf tip as shown in figure 4-29. That's enough work on this section for now.

Next work on refining the section on the other side of this one. Isolate the leaf tip as shown in figure 4-30. Bevel a ramp into the bottom of the leaf tip as shown in figure 4-31.

The next element to work on is the ribbon that flows into this leaf tip. The ribbon is a sequence of up-and-down rolling hills and valleys. To start the ribbon, use a #9 5 mm gouge to make the two cuts shown in figure 4-32. Note that the bottom of the troughs are about 1/16" from the back. Next draw pencil lines as shown in figure 4-33. These marks are where the high points will be. Use the #9 5 mm gouge to cut troughs between the marks as shown in figure 4-34. Now use a flat chisel to round over the edges of the troughs to form the hills. Figure 4-35 shows the result. Use a small, round file or scraper to blend most of the facets. The surface doesn't need to be perfect because accent marks will be cut later. This element is done for now.

Next work on the leaf cluster as shown in figure 4-36. Use a V-tool to separate the leaves as shown. Note the black lines. These will be used shortly. Remove the material on the leaf tips as shown in figure 4-37. This makes the leaves fold down, which is the desired effect. Note how close the leaf tip is above the C-scroll. Use a #9 10 mm gouge to make the cut shown in figure 4-38. Note how the cut flows into the leaf tip, but doesn't impact it. The limits of this cut are the black lines noted before. Also note how close the cut comes to the bottom. Cutting close to the edge of the blank gives a light and delicate appearance.

Continue shaping the leaves in this cluster by rounding over the back edges of the two tips just separated. Figures 4-39 and 4-40 show early and intermediate progress on one of the tips. Mark the tip detail as shown and cut it with a #7 4 mm gouge. Figure 4-41 shows the result.

Now implement the same treatment on the adjacent leaf. Figure 4-42 shows the rounded backside and the tip detail drawn. Figure 4-43 shows the finished leaf. The third leaf in the same area is scooped instead of rounded. Leaf "A" in figure 4-44 is the one that is scooped. Use a #9 10 mm gouge for this.

Figure 4-37. Separate the leaf tips.

Figure 4-38. Use a #9 gouge to scoop out the interior of the C-scroll. Feather it out just before the leaf tip.

Figure 4-39. Further define the separate leaves.

Figure 4-40. Detail the leaf as before with a #7 4 mm gouge.

Figure 4-41. The leaf detail is complete.

Figure 4-42. Add the same detail in the leaf just above the C-scroll.

Figure 4-43. The leaf detail is complete.

Figure 4-44. Scoop the leaf using a #9 10 mm gouge.

Figure 4-45. Shape the inner portion of the C-scroll.

APPLIED PIERCED VINE

While in this same area, further refine the neighboring C-scroll. Draw the lines as shown in figure 4-45. Use a #7 6 mm gouge to set in along the button extensions and use a #9 5 mm or 7 mm gouge to scoop the section between the buttons. Figure 4-46 shows the result. This will take a few iterations and cutting from both directions to achieve smooth, crisp edges.

Now work on the top cluster as shown in figure 4-47. Use a #9 10 mm or 13 mm gouge to scoop the leaf in the foreground labeled "A." Start at the leaf tip and blend into the previous cut as you progress down the stem. As the stem narrows, switch to a smaller gouge.

Separate the second leaf tip by setting in along line "B" in figure 4-47. Bevel into this stop cut from above. Use a #7 10 mm gouge to scoop the other leaf in a similar manner. Blend this cut into the stem with a narrow #9. Note how one edge of the scoop cut for leaf "B" forms the ridge "C." Further note how ridge "C" flows into leaf tip "D."

Leaf "D" is rounded over with a convex surface from ridge "C" on the backside as it flows into leaf "B," and there is a concave surface on the other side of "C" as it blends into the stem. There is also a secondary leaf tip detail in the concave portion. It is the same detail that is on the other leaves that is formed with a stop cut using a #7 4 mm gouge and then beveling into it. Figure 4-48 shows another view of this area.

There are a couple of leaves on the inside surface of the stalk. Figure 4-49 shows the layout and figure 4-50 shows the leaves. Form these by isolating the tips and then scooping each leaf individually.

What remains is to add some accent lines and decorative holes. Form the holes in the C-scroll with a nail set as shown in figure 4-46. Be careful not to fracture the scroll with the nail set. Figure 4-51 shows the completed vine. Study this picture for the other accent lines. Use a #11 2 mm gouge for these.

Figure 4-46. Use a #9 7 mm gouge to scoop the inside of the scroll and terminate into the ends.

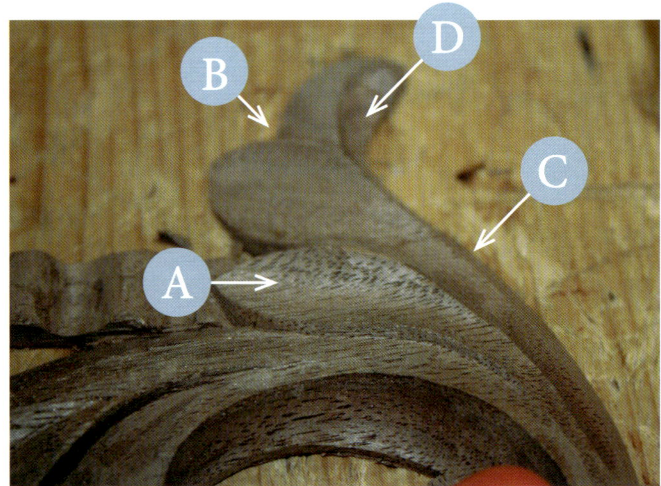

Figure 4-47. Refine the various leaves on the upper cluster.

Figure 4-48. The completed upper cluster from a different angle.

Figure 4-49. There is another leaf tucked into one side of the cutout.

Figure 4-50. Separate the leaf tip and use a #7 gouge to scoop it.

Figure 4-51. The vine is completely shaped. What remains are accent lines and punch holes.

5 OGEE BRACKET FEET: STANDARD AND BLOCKED

Ogee bracket feet were used on case furniture of all sizes in the eighteenth century. The ogee, or S-curve, is a refinement from straight bracket feet and is found on later pieces. There are many variations of the form, with the common element being the S-curve in the vertical cross section. The differences are in the depth of the S-shape and the profile toward the narrow end.

Figure 5-1. *Photo by Ramon Moreno.*

Figure 5-2.

On the Newport block front furniture of the Townsends and Goddards, there is an additional embellishment; the blocking is carried down into the bracket foot. Thus in addition to the ogee curve, there is another level in the front-to-back profile that follows the blocking of the elements above it. An additional refinement is a carved button that terminates the blocked portion of the foot. Figures 5-1 and 5-2 show some common examples.

This chapter describes how to shape two examples of an ogee bracket foot. The first one is sized for a tall case clock or small chest, which is a very common usage. The second one is sized and designed for a John Townsend Newport block front kneehole bureau table. It will include a carved button, which is a very elegant addition. At first glance the blocked ogee foot looks quite intimidating. However, with closer inspection and study it can be clearly understood as a series of relatively simple steps.

The first foot is more straightforward than the blocked one, but the techniques used on the simpler one are completely transferable to the other. Said another way, the blocked one is a lot like the simpler one with a couple of added steps.

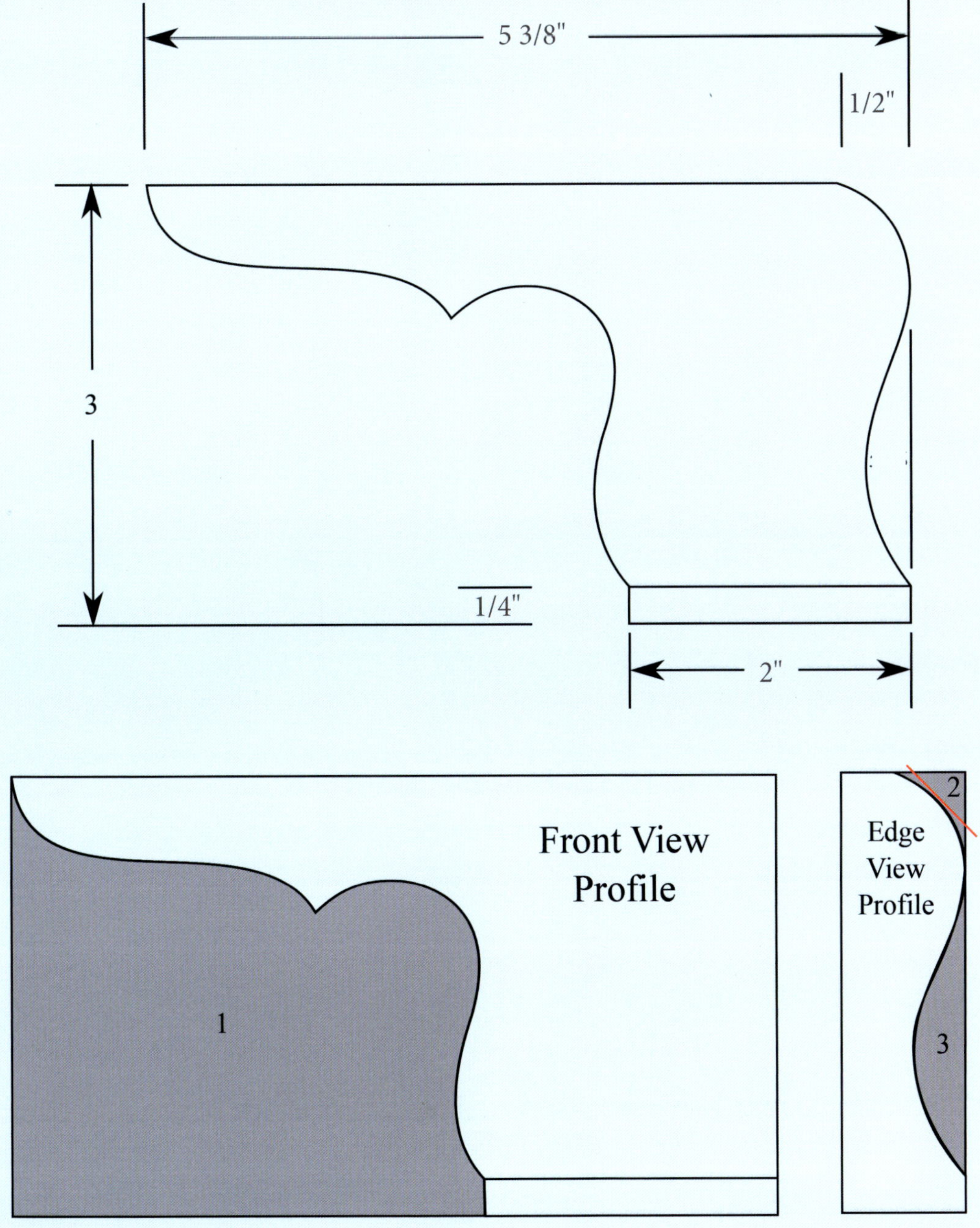

Figure 5-3. Ogee bracket foot sized for a tall case clock. The top drawing shows the dimensions and the finished profile of the ogee bracket foot. The bottom two drawings show the cutting sequence that will produce one-half of an ogee bracket foot. First cut the front view profile with a bandsaw. This removes the section labeled "1". Then shape the edge view profile with rasps, files, carving gouges, and scrapers. Remove the section labeled "2" with a #49 pattern maker's rasp. Rough out the section labeled "3" with #7 20 mm carving gouge and blend the remaining facets with a French curve-shaped scraper. The forward ogee curve will be formed when the foot blank is mitered at 45°.

OGEE BRACKET FOOT BLOCK

The way that I make ogee bracket feet is a little unconventional in that I cut the back portion of the front profile first and then I shape the ogee curve. With this method it is easy to overlap foot blanks to conserve wood or use odd-shaped blanks that might otherwise be scrap. Start by making a template from figure 5-3. This template has both the front and edge profiles. Note that six blanks are needed for a typical project. Two blanks are needed for each of the front feet and one for each of the back feet. The front feet pieces are mirror images, mitered and backed with secondary wood. The second piece for a back foot is a piece of secondary wood and can be dovetailed to its mate.

Figure 5-3 also shows the sequence of steps that will be used to form and shape one foot blank. Transfer the front face profile to an appropriately sized piece of wood about ⅞" thick. The thickness is not critical as long as it is thick enough to accommodate the edge profile with a little to spare. In this case ¾" is about the minimum required. Figure 5-4 shows the profile transferred to the blank along with some layout lines. These layout lines carry the high and low points of the ogee and the location of the fillet the length of the blank. The line for the high point and the fillet will remain until the very end, and the line for the low point will guide the carving gouge to cut a straight trough.

Next cut the face profile using a band saw. With two feet overlapped, separate the two blanks before cutting to the line. These sequences are shown in figures 5-5 and 5-6. Clean up the band saw marks on the edge with a small half-round file.

Use a square to transfer the trough line down the edge on the other side. Make a mark on the edge line 5/16" from the top. This is the depth of the S-curve. Figure 5-7 shows this layout. Next transfer the front edge profile to the front edge and extend the line on the top edge as shown in figure 5-8. The line on top is ½" from the front face and extends the top point of the front profile. The blank is now ready to be shaped.

There are two portions that need to be removed. They are shown in figure 5-3. Start with the section labeled "2" because it is a little easier to clamp the blank before the concave area is carved. With your finger as a guide, draw lines on the top and front surfaces ¼" from the edge. Figure 5-9 shows the technique and results. The strategy to rounding over the top corner will be to bevel between the guide lines and then blend from the middle of the beveled surface to the edge lines on both the top and front.

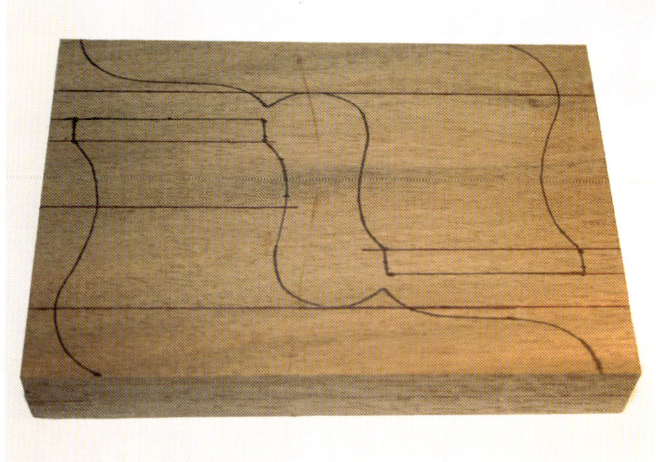

Figure 5-4. Position two feet for more efficient use of the stock. Mark the high and low areas of the foot.

Figure 5-5. Rough cut the feet apart.

Figure 5-6. Cut the back side portion of the front profile.

Figure 5-7. Mark the depth of the cove portion of the foot. This is 5⁄16" from the front face.

Figure 5-8. Draw the side profile on the edge.

Figure 5-9. Draw a guide line ¼" from the top and front along the length of the foot.

Figure 5-10. Use a #49 rasp to create a bevel between the two lines just drawn.

Clamp the blank to a flat surface and use a #49 pattern maker's rasp to bevel between the two guidelines. Be aggressive with this cut, especially in the beginning, and the operation will go quite fast. Using the same #49, round from the centerline of the beveled surface to both the profile edge line on the top and the high point line on the front. Figures 5-10 and 5-11, respectively, show intermediate progress and the operation complete. Stay a little proud of the perimeter lines with the #49 and ease into them with a file. This will yield a straighter and more refined line. The goal is to create a smooth, continuous, and round surface between the two perimeter lines. At this stage the high point line on the front face should be visible. This will be blended away as a last cleanup step.

Now carve the concave section labeled "3" in figure 5-3. Use a #7 20 mm gouge to carve a trough with the line centered in the cut. With the same gouge, deepen the cut along this line to the depth marks made on each end. On the front end this will be the profile curve, and on the back end this will be the mark made 5⁄16" down from the front surface. Figure 5-12 shows the beginning and figure 5-13 shows progress after a couple of iterations. Carve to the profile curve on the front end and carry these cuts to the back end. This will create a uniform trough from front to back. Carve close to the fillet line, but stay a little proud. Figure 5-14 shows the gouge cuts complete. Use a flat chisel to remove the corner on the convex portion. Figure 5-15 shows the result. Now clean up the facets to get a smooth, uniform, and continuous surface. Use your hand to feel for any irregularities. I use a French curve scraper, files, and sandpaper for cleanup. Sandpaper wrapped around a round backer as shown in figure 5-16 works great for the concave surface. A flat sanding block works well for the convex areas. Figure 5-17 shows the cleanup complete.

Assembling the foot comes next. If this is to be the visible portion of a back foot, there is no more to be done other than to join it to its mate. If this is to be for one of the front feet, then a second mirror-image piece is needed as well as a 45° miter at the front end of each piece. The S curve on the front edge will be created when the miter cut is made. For the front feet, leave a little extra length at the front edge so there is some margin to cut the miter. The back feet can be cut to the finished length before shaping.

Figure 5-11. Rasp the approximated surface to match the round profile as seen from the edge.

Figure 5-12. Clamp the foot in preparation for carving the cove portion of the ogee.

Figure 5-13. Use a wider #7 gouge to cut a trough. Follow the profile line on the front edge and match the depth to the mark made earlier.

Figure 5-16. Use a contoured sanding block with a rounded edge and 80-grit sandpaper to help blend the surface.

Figure 5-14. Carve close to the profile line.

Figure 5-17. After smoothing the ogee surface, the foot is ready to be joined to its mate.

Figure 5-15. Start to round the convex portion by removing the corner with a flat chisel.

Figure 5-18.

BLOCKED OGEE BRACKET FOOT: KNEEHOLE BUREAU TABLE

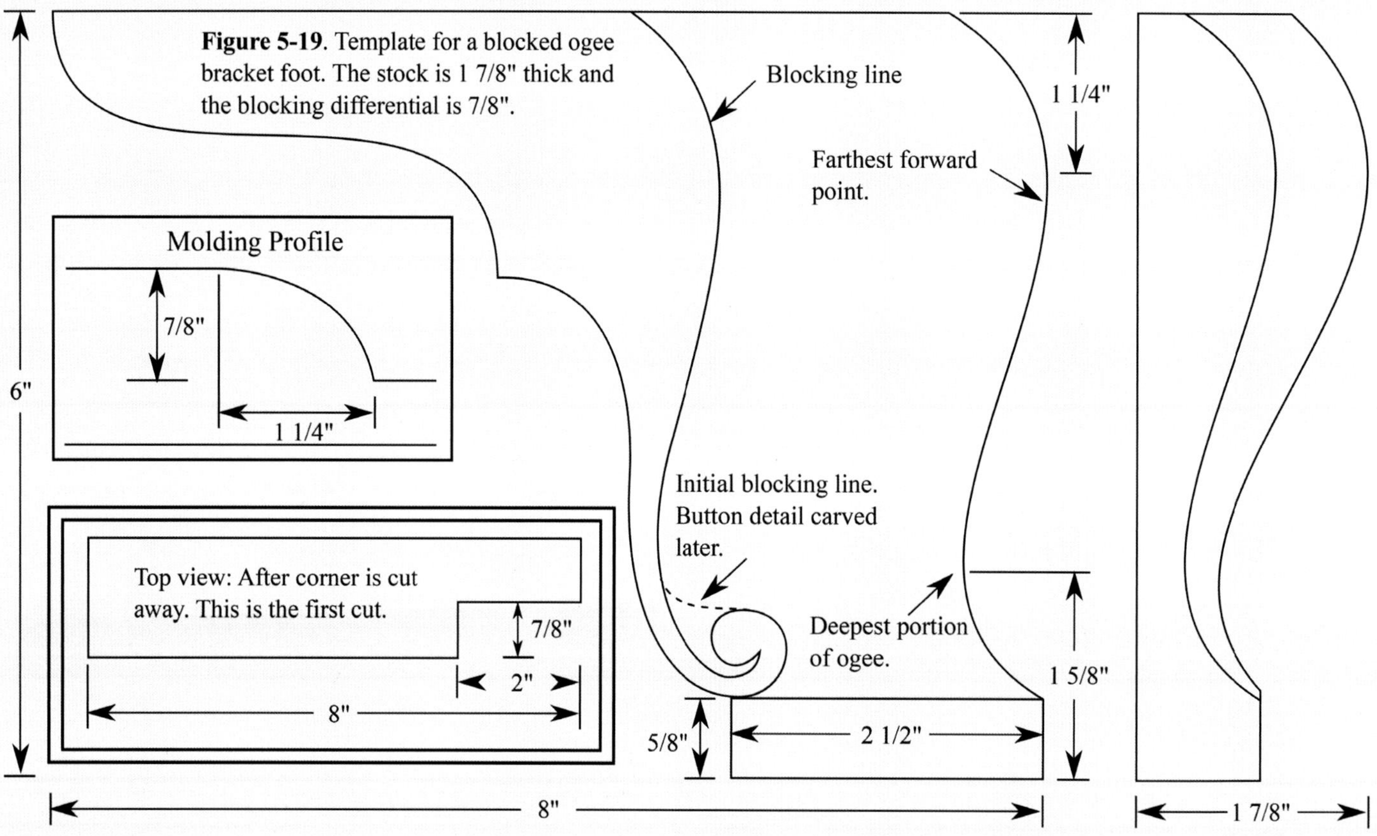

Figure 5-19.

A more elaborate version of an ogee bracket foot is found on the block front pieces of the Townsends and Goddards of Newport, Rhode Island. In this case, the blocking is carried into the foot. This detail adds a lot to the visual impact of the foot because it adds depth and heft. A carved terminating button adds even more elegance in the detail. The concepts and techniques for this foot are similar to the one just described with a few added steps. The one I am going to describe here is sized for a Newport kneehole bureau table. Figure 5-18 shows an example.

Start by making a template from figure 5-19. The only significant differences between this template and the simpler one are the size and the extra curve close to the back end. This line represents the blocked portion. Now transfer the front profile to a block of wood 1⅞" thick. The extra thickness is for the blocking. Figure 5-20 shows this profile transferred to the blank.

Next cut out the front face corner. This is the first step in establishing the blocked portion. The segment to remove is ⅞" deep, 2" wide, and 6" high. The width may be a little more depending on how much margin is added in the front. In this case the width is 2⅛". Use a marking gauge set to ⅞" to score a line around the three edges and use a knife and a square to mark the front, top, and bottom. Figure 5-21 shows these marks. Use a band saw to remove the corner. Figure 5-22 shows the corner removed.

Figure 5-20. Joint the top edge and transfer the template for the blocked foot to the blank.

Figure 5-21. Cut out the marked section with a band saw.

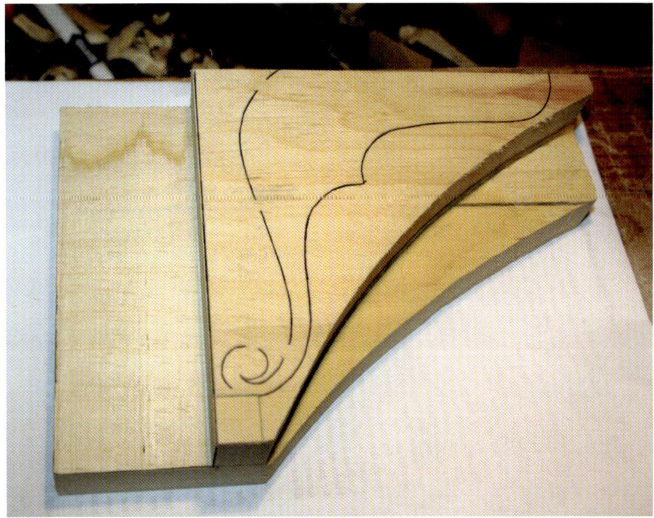

Figure 5-22. Progress after the band saw cut.

Figure 5-23. Use a large, flat chisel to get close to the line.

Next remove the material up to the blocking curve down to the ⅞" depth established when the corner was cut out. Approximate the curve with a flat chisel and mallet to remove most of the material, staying proud of the line. Figures 5-23 and 5-24 show early and late progress, respectively. Now use a flat chisel to extend the flat bottom into the curve as shown in figure 5-25. Finally, carve to the blocking line using #2, #3, and #5 gouges. Use a #7 10 mm gouge to carve around the button area. Extend the flat bottom surface into the curved wall. Figure 5-26 shows late progress and figure 5-27 shows the operation complete.

The block portion of the foot is now established. It needs more shaping before rounding the corner, but that will be done later. Next form the ogee in the front portion up to the blocked section in a similar manner as for the previous foot. Begin by drawing the edge profile on the front edge of the blank. Draw the lines shown in figure 5-28. These lines determine the heights and depths of the carved areas. Use a square to draw these lines.

Start by rounding over the top portion. Draw the additional lines shown in figure 5-29 and use a flat chisel to cut a bevel between them. Figure 5-30 shows progress creating the bevel. Complete the rounding with the flat chisel and blend the facets with a file. Figure 5-31 shows the result.

Figure 5-24. Use a large #9 gouge to remove material in the curved area.

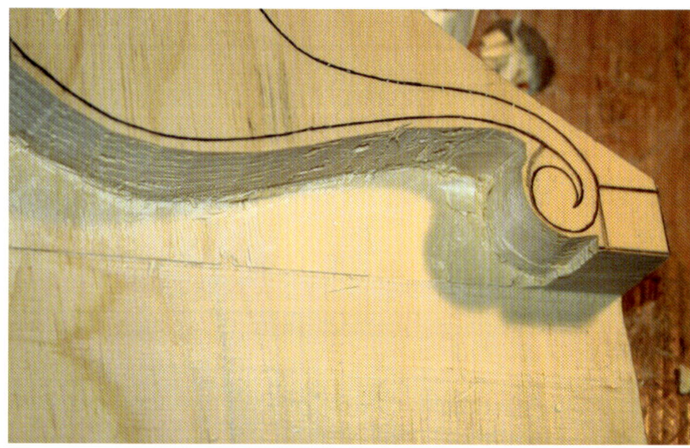

Figure 5-25. The approximation is complete.

Figure 5-26. Cut to the profile line using a flat chisel along the convex curves and appropriate sweep gouges along the concave ones.

Figure 5-27. Make the vertical wall along the curve meet the background at a right angle.

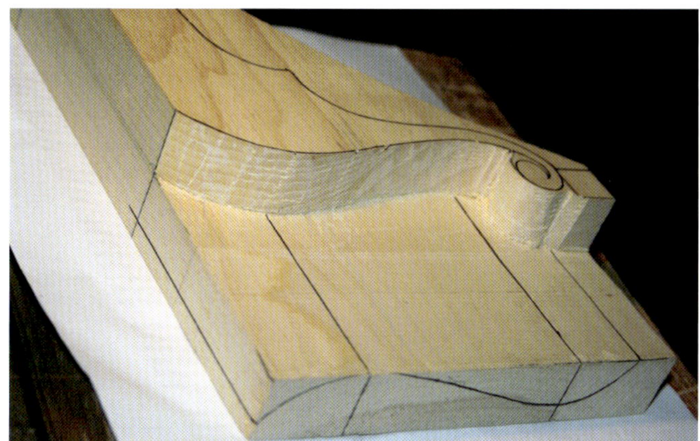

Figure 5-28. Draw the edge profile as shown and mark the high and low spots using a square.

Figure 5-29. The marked corner is to approximate the convex shape of the top portion.

Figure 5-30. Remove the corner with a chisel and/or a rasp.

Figure 5-31. Round the corner to the edge profile.

Now carve the concave section. Use a #7 20 mm gouge to carve along the trough line. Figure 5-32 shows progress after a few cuts. Use a flat chisel to carve the convex section as shown in figure 5-33. Continue in this manner until the entire front profile is sculpted. Use a square registered against the front edge to verify the depth is correct along the entire length of the base surface. Figure 5-34 shows this technique. Figure 5-35 shows the ogee surface complete. The vertical wall will need to be extended as the concave surface is established. Strive to make the wall and the ogee surface meet at a right angle the entire length. It doesn't have to be perfect now because it can be corrected when the wall is rounded.

At this point the front portion of the foot is shaped and complete. Conceptually it is the same as the front portion of the simpler foot. The next step is to cut along the back profile using a band saw. Figure 5-36 shows the result. Now further shape the blocked portion prior to rounding the curved edge and carving the button. The strategy to shaping the blocked section is similar to shaping the ogee on the front portion.

Because this foot will be below a blocked base molding, the profile of that molding needs to be drawn on the top edge of the foot. Make a template from the base molding profile shown in figure 5-19 and transfer it to the top edge of the foot. Figure 5-37 shows the transfer. Also draw the high point line on the blocked section 1¼" down from the top. This line is also shown in figure 5-37.

Use the #49 rasp to round over the top corner from the high point line to the edge profile line on the top. Start by beveling a flat surface and then blend from the middle of this surface to the terminating lines. Strive for a uniform, smooth, and continuous curved surface. Stay a little proud of the terminating lines with the rasp and blend to them with a smoother file. Figure 5-38 shows intermediate progress and figure 5-39 shows the work complete.

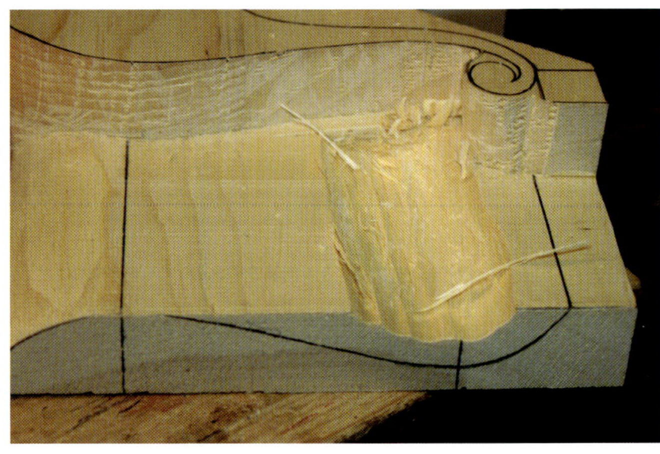

Figure 5-32. Use a larger #7 gouge to cut a trough as was previously done for the smaller foot.

Figure 5-33. Use a flat chisel to carry the profile curve all the way to the curved vertical wall.

Figure 5-34. The ogee surface should be square to the curved vertical wall at every point. Use a square to determine where material needs to be removed.

Figure 5-35. The ogee curve has been smoothed and blended with files, scrapers, and sandpaper.

Figure 5-36. Cut along the back front profile line using a band saw.

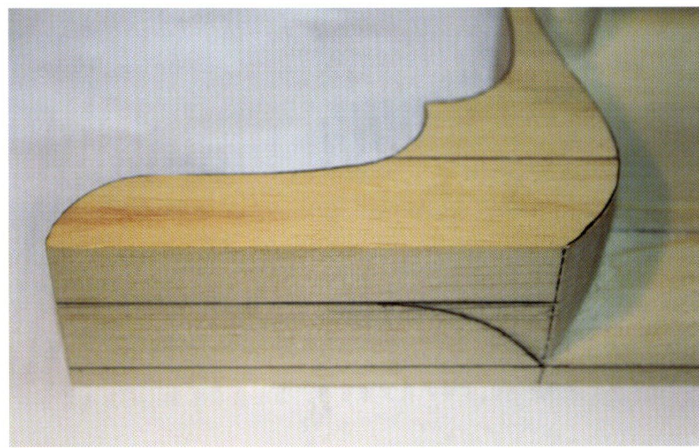

Figure 5-37. Use the molding profile template and transfer it as shown.

Figure 5-38. Use a #49 rasp to start rounding the top portion of the blocked section.

Figure 5-39. The top portion is sufficiently rounded for now.

The next operation is to shape the lower portion of the blocked section so that it follows the S-curve of the ogee. The very bottom of the blocking element is below the level of the fillet and follows the concave portion of the ogee curve. To get close to the desired shape, quickly use a flat chisel to lower the lower section. Figure 5-40 shows early progress. Use the same flat chisel to extend the fillet as shown in figure 5-41. The button area is below the fillet, so establish this now.

Next blend the height of the blocked section with a flowing curve from the high point line to the button area. Use the #49 rasp for this operation. The curve is convex near the high point line and transitions to concave as it enters the ogee area. Figure 5-42 shows intermediate progress. The line in figure 5-43 shows the desired flow and depth. Continue rasping to this line. Figure 5-44 shows the result.

This is the desired shape of the blocked section. It's now time to define the button. Use the template to draw the button as shown in figure 5-45. Note how the button return line flows into the wall as it moves up the ogee curve. Use a #7 10 mm gouge to set in around the tight curve of the button. Use flatter gouges to blend the return into the wall. Make the sides of the button perpendicular to the surface. Figure 5-46 shows the button established. During this operation you will probably find that the ogee background surface needs to be lowered around the button. This is normal and expected. Use your eyes and finger to see where the ogee surface needs blending. The goal is to have the button sitting on top of a uniform ogee surface. It is difficult to access the ogee surface between the button and the block wall. A small, flat chisel such as a #1 1 mm and 3 mm will help.

Next round over the blocked section. Start at the top corner shown in figure 5-47. Use a ¾" flat chisel for most of the rounding. The facets will then be blended with a file. The goal is to round the corner from the background surface up to the height of the blocked section and follow the curve of the molding outline drawn on the top. Figures 5-48 and 5-49 show early and intermediate progress.

Figure 5-40. The button follows the shape of the ogee. Begin to bring that portion closer to the background surface.

Figure 5-41. More progress lowering the button area.

Figure 5-42. Still more progress in the button area.

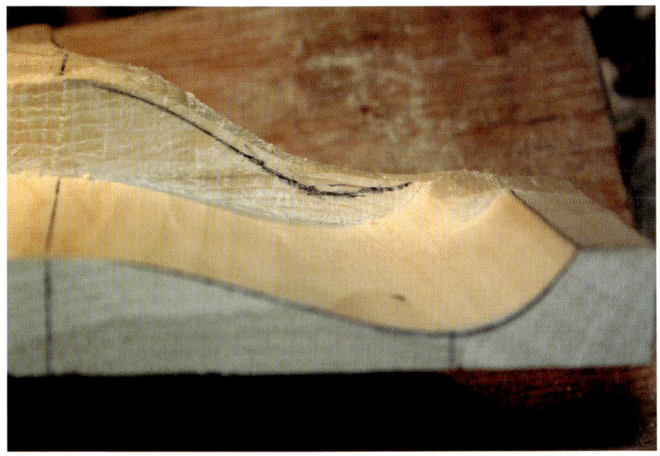

Figure 5-43. The line shows the curve that the block portion should follow. Note that the curve falls off from the high point previously drawn.

Figure 5-44. The button area is properly shaped.

Figure 5-45. Draw in the button as shown. Connect the button with a smooth curve.

Figure 5-46. Use a #7 6 mm gouge to set in around the button along the tighter curve and a #5 along the outside. Note that the background surrounding the button is also a curve, so continue that surface when cutting into the button sides.

Figure 5-47. Round over the corner of the blocked section using the curve as a guide.

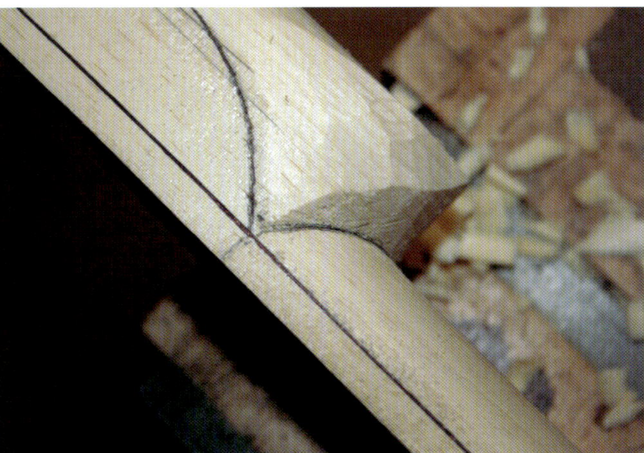

Figure 5-48. Use a flat chisel to remove the initial parts of the corner.

Continue with the flat chisel, rounding more of the corner and working down toward the button. Figure 5-50 shows more progress. Use the chisel with the bevel both up and down, depending on what works better. Also change the direction of the cuts as the grain changes. When part of the corner is removed, blend that cut into the surrounding surface. This will guide how far to extend the blending into the front of the blocked surface. If any portion of the blocked wall is perpendicular to the ogee surface, that angle should be made greater than 90°. This is also visible in figure 5-50. The rounded, blocked section should not have the appearance of just a rounded corner. If this is the case, not enough material has been removed. The goal is to have a curve that looks more like a circle than a rounded rectangle.

When the entire corner has been removed with the flat chisel, use a file to blend the facets. Strive for a continuously flowing surface. Your eye should not see any facets, nor should your hand feel any. Figure 5-51 shows a nicely smoothed surface.

Finally, round the edges of the button slightly as shown in figure 5-52. Use a flat chisel or a #2 8 mm gouge.

Some things to strive for when carving this foot are to create crisp, flowing curves for the surface intersections. Figure 5-53 shows an example. There is a pleasing, crisp line that is the intersection of the blocked section and the convex portion of the ogee foot. There is also a single point of intersection where the molding profile line meets the blocked section. These kind of details will elevate your work above the norm.

This portion of the foot is now complete. What remains is to miter the front edge at 45° and join it to its mate. Note that only the front half is blocked. The other half does not have blocking and is shaped exactly like the smaller foot described at the beginning of this chapter. The stock for the non-blocked half should just be as thick as the ogee background portion of the blocked half.

Figure 5-49. More progress with the flat chisel.

Figure 5-50. Further progress with the flat chisel. Even though there are many facets, the overall curve is quite visible.

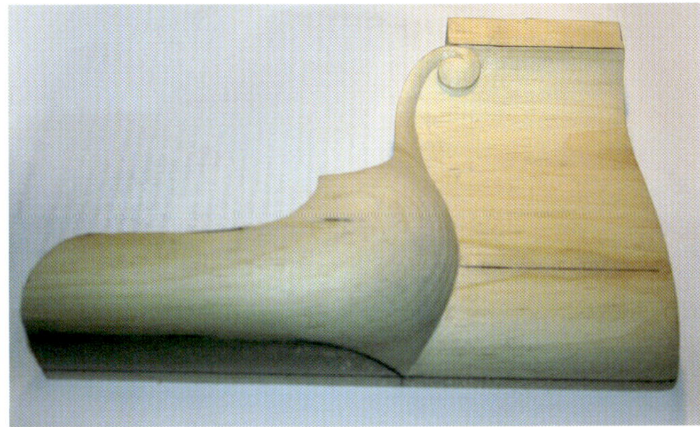

Figure 5-51. Smooth the corner with a file.

Figure 5-52. The button has a slight dome on it. Use a flat chisel to ease the corners slightly and blend the facets with a file and sandpaper.

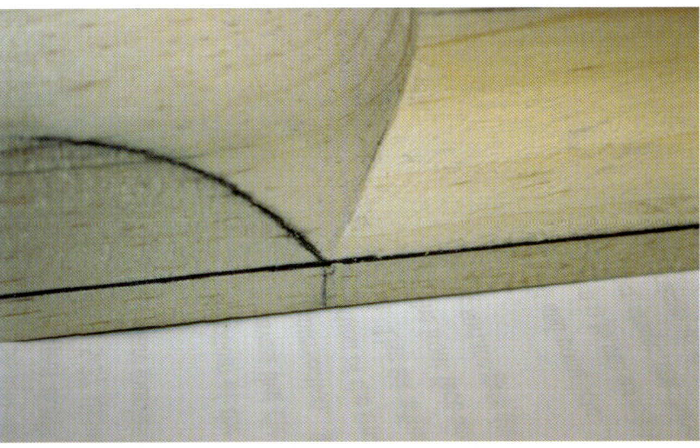

Figure 5-53. Strive for a crisp line that is the intersection of meeting surfaces. This is pleasing to the eye and is a sign of good craftsmanship.

Figure 5-54.

TRIFFID FOOT

A triffid foot is a three "toed" element that terminates a cabriole leg. There were several variations in shape and detail, but the common theme is that the foot is separated into three segments from side to side. Typically the toes have a raised "stocking" on top. This has the effect of separating and accentuating the toes as they blend into the ankle of the leg.

Figure 6-1.

Figure 6-2.

Figure 6-3.

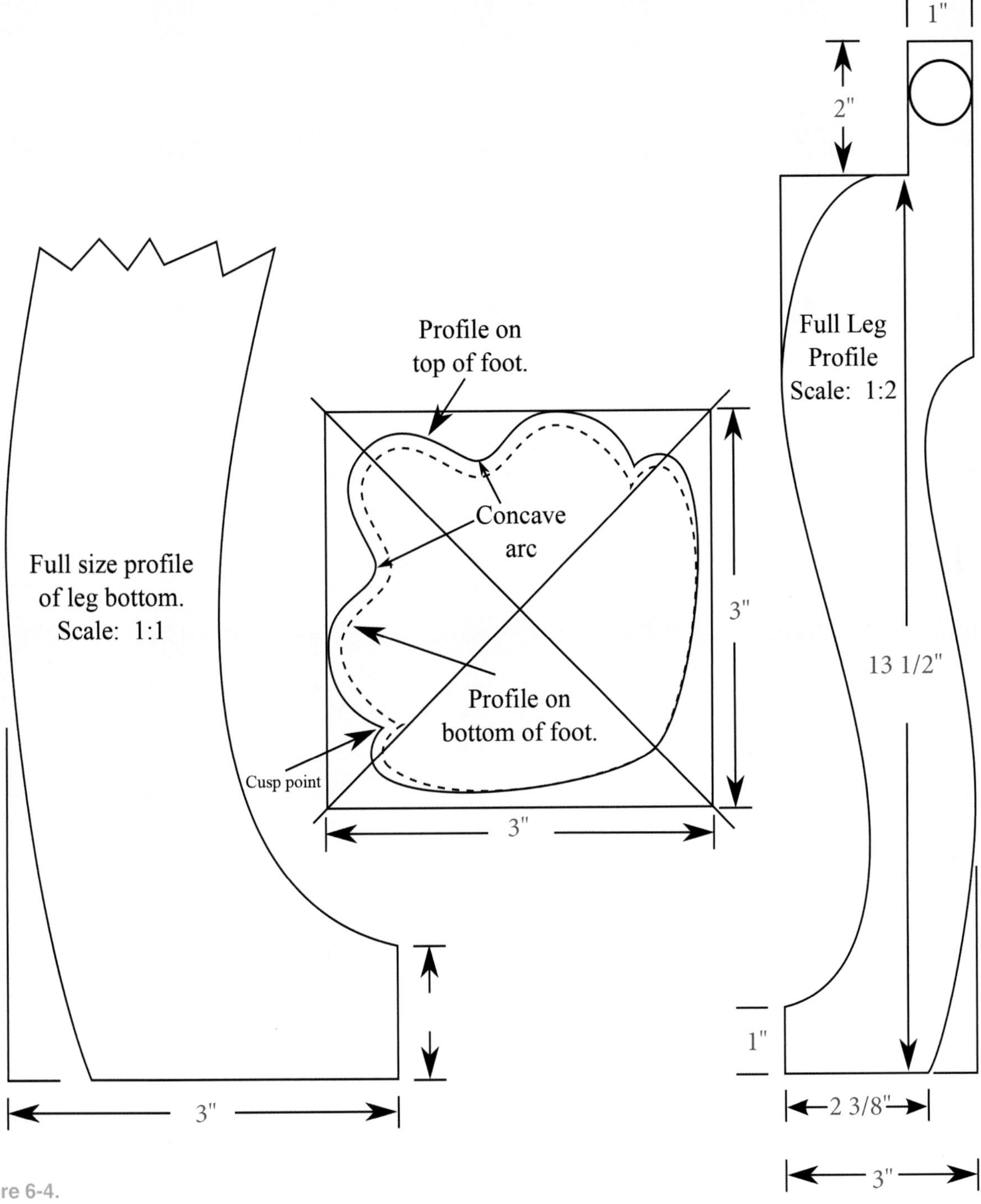

Figure 6-4.

The triffid foot was popular on Queen Anne furniture and rarely found on later pieces with Chippendale styling. It is more elaborate than a pad or slipper foot, but not as refined as a ball and claw. This refinement corresponds with the chronology of its use. As the eighteenth century progressed, the furniture styles and tastes evolved from form as the primary design attribute in the Queen Anne period to straighter lines with more elaborate carved decoration in the Chippendale era. As with all cultural advancements, there are no rigid boundaries and there is overlap, but this was generally the trend. The triffid foot is in the middle of the styling evolution. Figures 6-1 through 6-3 show some examples of the variations in the foot as well as the variety of its use. As you can see from the examples, this style of foot was used on the finest pieces of the time.

TRIFFID FOOT

From a carving viewpoint, a triffid foot is a lot less work than a ball and claw foot. However, some of the layout and initial processes are similar. The foot that I describe in this chapter is for the Queen Anne armchair shown in figure 6-1. Figure 6-4 shows the templates that will be needed for this foot. For completeness I have included a scaled version of the entire leg. I will not discuss shaping the cabriole leg here, but assume that has been done. To adapt this foot for a different piece of furniture, all that is needed is to draw the appropriate cabriole template for the desired height. The size of this foot will fit nicely on any of them.

Begin by making templates from the drawings in figure 6-4. Make one template that contains both foot profiles. This technique easily places the two profiles relative to each other. Figure 6-5 shows my template. Both of these profiles are drawn on the bottom of the foot blank. After the cabriole leg is cut and shaped, the strategy will be to first cut and carve to the top profile and then blend from this one to the bottom one.

Prepare a 3"-square leg blank of the appropriate height. Transfer the templates to the blank as shown in figure 6-6. Rough cut the cabriole shape using a band saw and shape the leg using rasps, files, and scrapers. For this foot, do not remove the bottom back corner with the band saw. That is the red line shown in figure 6-6. Remove the front and two side corners with a hand saw. Use the guidelines as shown in figure 6-7 to keep the cuts square to the blank. Figure 6-8 shows the corners removed.

Secure the blank in a vise as shown in figure 6-9. Round over the back side of the foot, blending the profile on the bottom into the ankle of the leg. The final surface should be smooth and continuous to the touch and eye. There should be no visible or tangible bumps. Start with a #49 or #50 pattern maker's rasp and shape close to the profile line on the foot bottom. Strive for a continuous and uniform surface. When the surface is pretty close to its final shape, switch to a medium-cut bastard file. The purpose of this step is to smooth and refine the surface and not to reshape it in a significant way. The rasp is used to shape and the file is used to smooth. Figure 6-10 shows progress after the rasping step and figure 6-11 shows the final surface after filing.

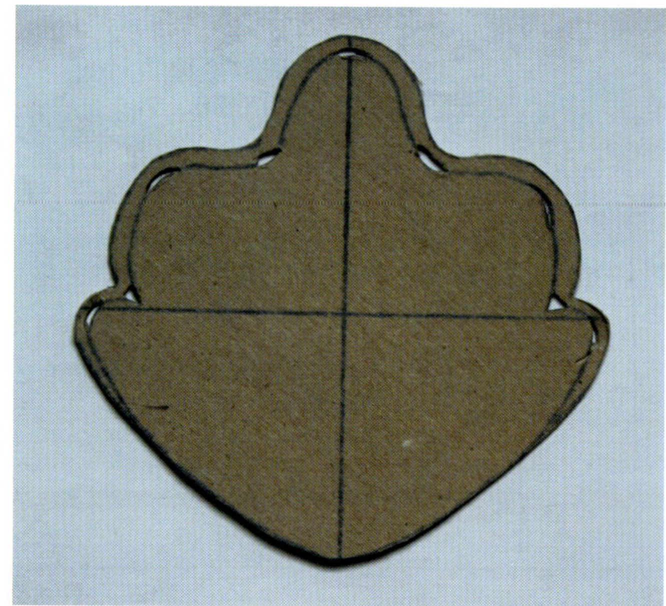

Figure 6-5.

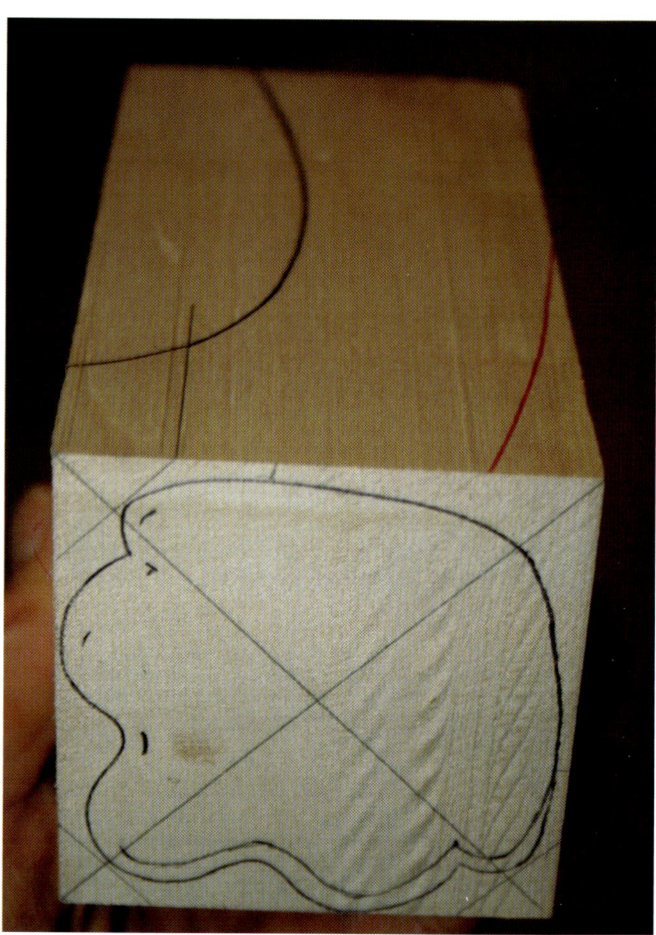

Figure 6-6. The bottom profiles transferred to the blank. Note which is the back and which is the front. Do not remove the red line with a band saw; this will remove too much material.

Figure 6-7. After the leg is cut from the blank, remove the corners with a hand saw.

Figure 6-8. The saw work is complete and the foot is ready for hand shaping and carving.

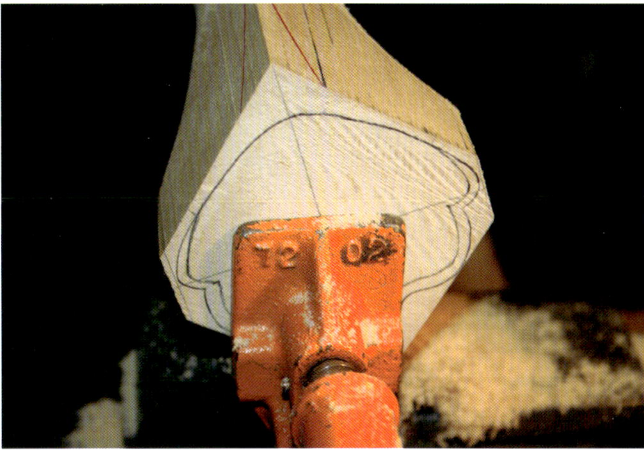

Figure 6-9. Clamp the leg and shape the back corner first.

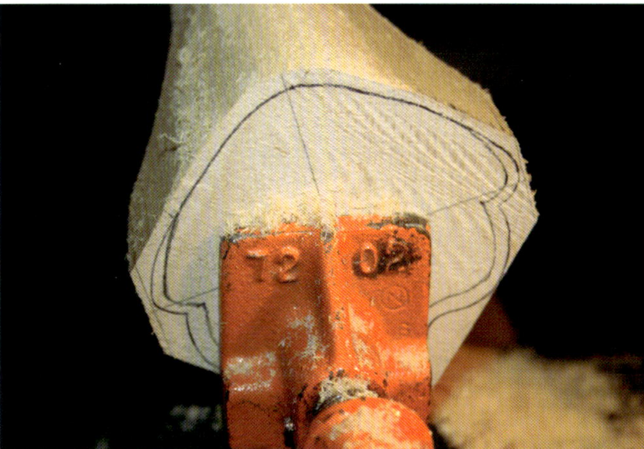

Figure 6-10. Use a #49 rasp to shape the back corner to the profile on the bottom. Feather the cut out 3" or 4" up the ankle.

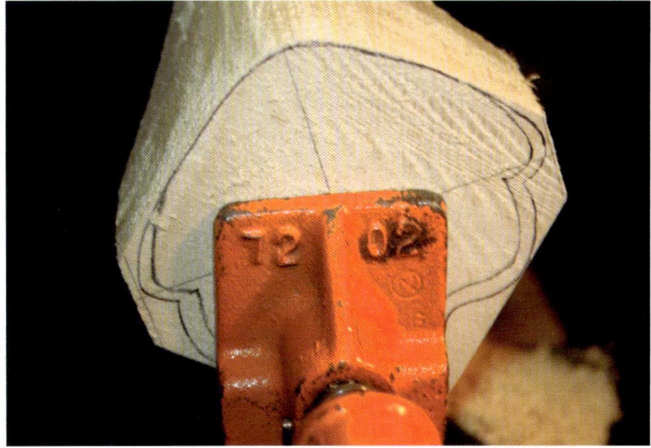

Figure 6-11. The back corner is mostly shaped. Get close to the line and come as far forward as the profile allows.

As a guide, draw a line on the side of the foot blank that extends the centerline of the concave arc on the foot bottom. This line is a guide for carving so that the profile on the bottom can be squarely transferred to the top of the foot. Figure 6-12 shows this line. Position the blank in the vise so that the concave portion between the front toe and one of the side toes is facing up. With a #9 15 mm gouge centered on the line just drawn, carve from the top of the foot to the bottom. Depending on the grain, switch directions and carve from the bottom to the top. Repeat with the #9, working to the depth of the "top of foot" profile. As the carved trough gets deeper, round over the walls with a flat chisel. Repeat this process until the profile is reached and this segment is complete. Figure 6-13 shows progress after a couple of iterations. The goal is to carve a vertical surface that follows the "top" profile as drawn on the foot bottom and is square to the sides the entire length of the profile. This transfers the "top" profile to the top of the foot, which is the objective. Check this with a square referenced from the bottom. Remove material until the vertical surface is perpendicular to the bottom. Figure 6-14 shows this section complete.

Using similar techniques, carve the adjacent segment toward the back of the foot. Use a V-tool to cut along the line extension of the cusp point. Figure 6-15 shows this cut. With a flat chisel, carve to the profile on either side of the V-cut. Repeat these steps until just proud of the outside profile. Use a file to finish shaping to the outside profile and blending into the ankle of the leg. Figure 6-16 shows half of the foot completed.

Repeat this process on the other half of the foot. At this point the foot should be shaped to the "top" (outer) profile with square sides up to the top of the foot. Figure 6-17 shows this operation complete.

Next carve a beveled surface down the sides from the top of the foot and terminating into the inner profile on the bottom. Leave the profile on the top untouched and cut progressively deeper moving toward the bottom. The goal is to make an angled straight line from the top profile to the bottom one along the entire perimeter of the profile curve. Use a #9 or #8 gouge for the concave portions and a flat chisel for the convex ones. Smooth the facets left from the carving with a small half-round file. Use the flat side for the convex portions and the half-round side for the concave ones. Figure 6-18 shows the result. At this point the shaping of the foot is complete. What remains is to separate the toes.

Figure 6-12. Mark the low spots and transfer these points up the foot with a square. These guides will help keep the side surfaces square to the bottom.

Figure 6-13. Use a #9 15 mm gouge to cut to the depth of the profile. Keep the cuts square to the bottom.

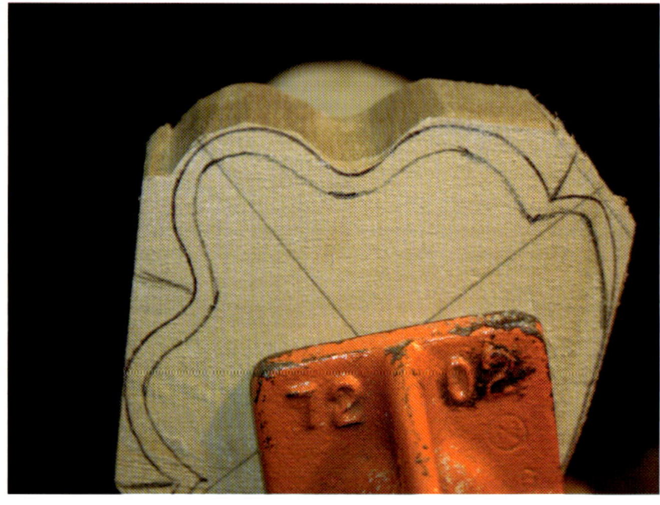

Figure 6-14. Round the convex portions with a flat chisel.

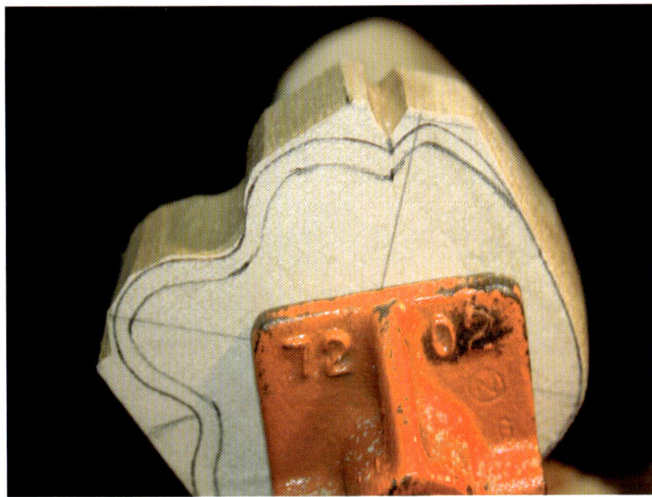

Figure 6-15. Use a V-tool to cut along the cusp line.

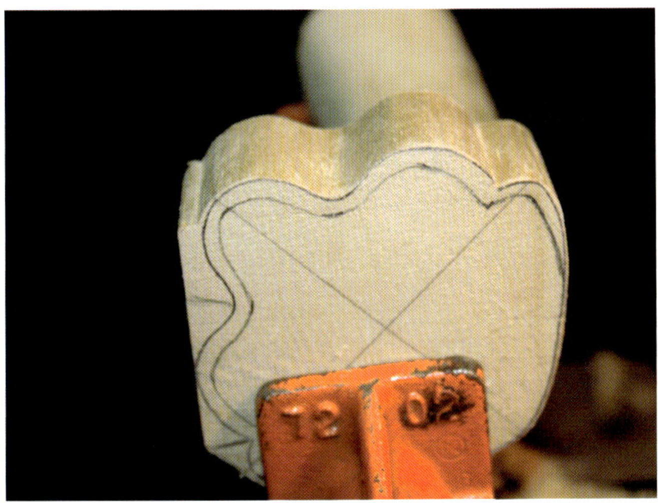

Figure 6-16. Use a file to form a smooth and uniform surface along the entire line of the profile.

Figure 6-17. The foot is shaped to the outside profile. From the top of the foot carve a bevel.

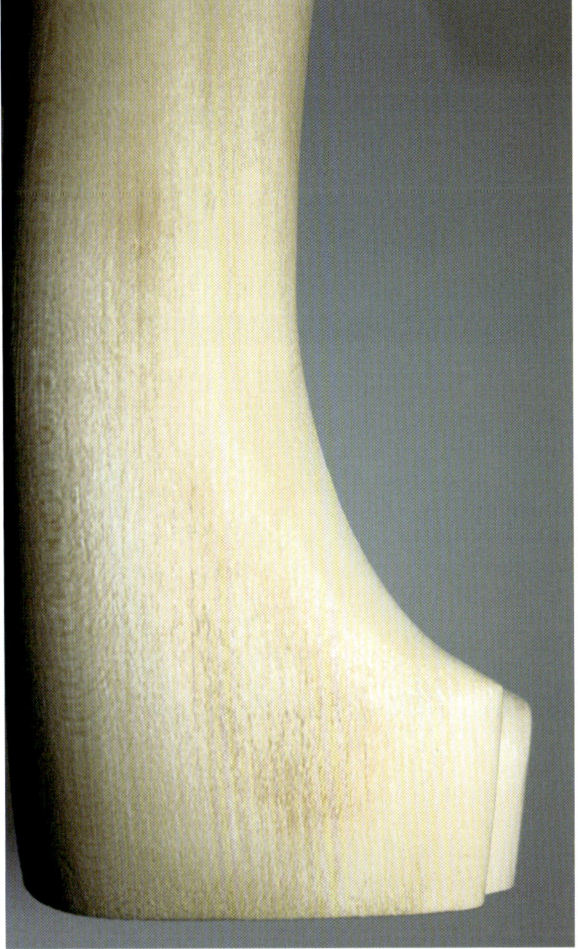

Figure 6-18. The foot sides are angled down to the inside profile on the bottom. Note the angle of the front edge going from top to bottom.

TRIFFID FOOT

On this foot, the toes are separated by recessing the ones on either side of the center toe. Start by drawing layout lines to delineate the toes. The top of the recess is about 5" off the ground and each side toe is approximately ⅜" wide. The width of the center toe at the top is ½" and it is centered on the ankle. The intersection of the height line and the center toe width is a point of reference. Draw a straight line on each side of the center toe, connecting this point with the side of the central toe where it protrudes. Figure 6-19 shows the lines separating the toes. These lines are drawn freehand using the measurements shown in the figure. Carve on the outside of the line defining the middle toe. Start on top of the foot at the end of the toe and carve off the end using a #9 10 mm gouge. Deepen the trough with two or three iterations and then move up the ankle a little and blend into the previous cut. Use narrower #9 gouges as the cuts progress up the ankle. Round over the edge of the side toe with a ½" flat chisel. As the cuts progress up the ankle, the depth gets shallower and very little wood needs to be removed to achieve the desired result. Do not round over the edge on the center toe side of the trough. This will give a crisp line defining the center toe. Figure 6-20 shows early progress.

The separation on the other side of this toe is a rounded corner that terminates in a vertical wall. Use a V-tool to carve along the inside of the separation line. Start toward the bottom of the toe and carve off the end of the foot. Move up the ankle a little and blend into the previous cut, deepening the trough toward the front of the foot. Repeat in this manner until reaching the top of the carved section. As the V-cut deepens, round over the side toe edge to allow easier access for the V-tool. Figure 6-21 shows the V-cut. Round over the top of the toe between these cuts so the surface is smooth and uniform.

The last step to complete the side toe is to separate the top of the toe from the ankle and round over the edge on the toe side. Use a V-tool to make the separation cut. Repeat these steps to define and detail the other side toe. Figure 6-22 shows the completed triffid foot.

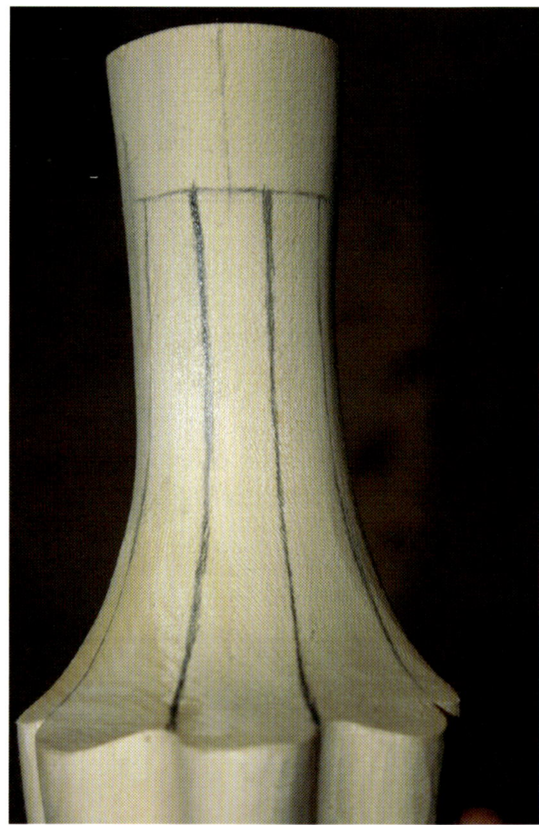

Figure 6-19. Define the center toe, both width and height.

Figure 6-20. Use #9 gouges to raise the center toe on each side.

Figure 6-21. Use a V-tool to separate the side toe from the back one.

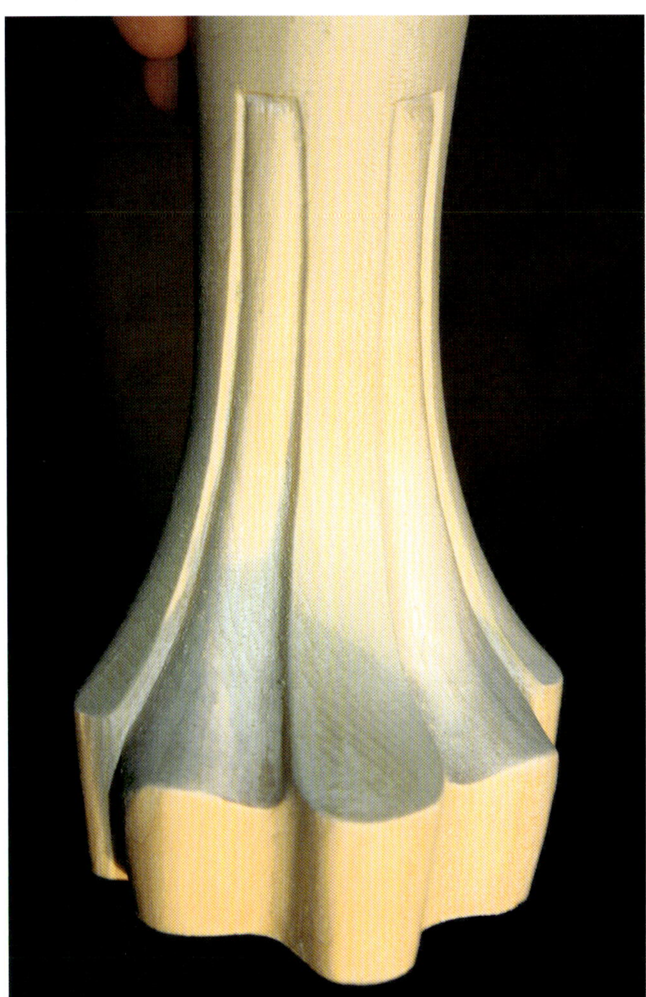

Figure 6-22. Round over the edges of the side toe. Smooth the toe surface. The foot is now complete.

PHILADELPHIA CHIPPENDALE CHAIR CARVED CREST RAIL

Philadelphia Chippendale and Queen Anne chairs are similar in style and construction, but there are three main stylistic differences: the crest rail, the seat frame, and the vertical lines of the back legs. There are two construction differences: how the seat frame is joined together and how the front legs are joined to the seat frame. I will not discuss these details here because that is not the focus of this chapter. However, a little discussion is valuable to add context.

Figure 7-1.

Figure 7-2.

Figure 7-3.

Figure 7-4.

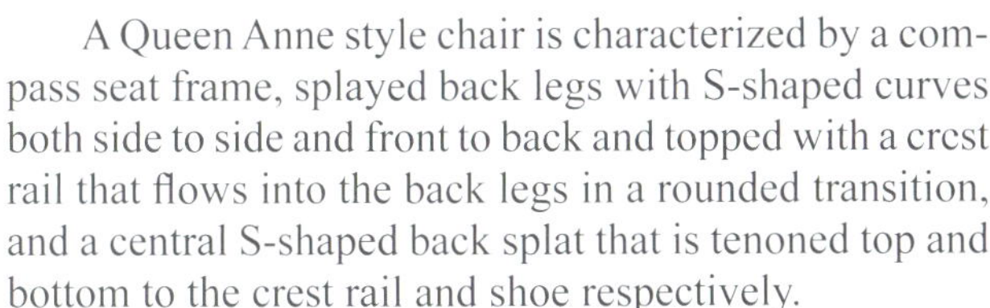

A Queen Anne style chair is characterized by a compass seat frame, splayed back legs with S-shaped curves both side to side and front to back and topped with a crest rail that flows into the back legs in a rounded transition, and a central S-shaped back splat that is tenoned top and bottom to the crest rail and shoe respectively.

In contrast, Philadelphia Chippendale style chairs are characterized by trapezoidal seat frames, splayed back legs that are straight side to side and C-shaped front to back and topped with a crest rail that is proud of the back legs on both sides, and a central C-shaped back splat that is tenoned in the same manner as the Queen Anne chair. Figures 7-1 and 7-2 show examples of typical Philadelphia Queen Anne chairs. Figures 7-3 and 7-4 are examples of typical Philadelphia Chippendale chairs. Note the differences as described.

Figure 7-5.

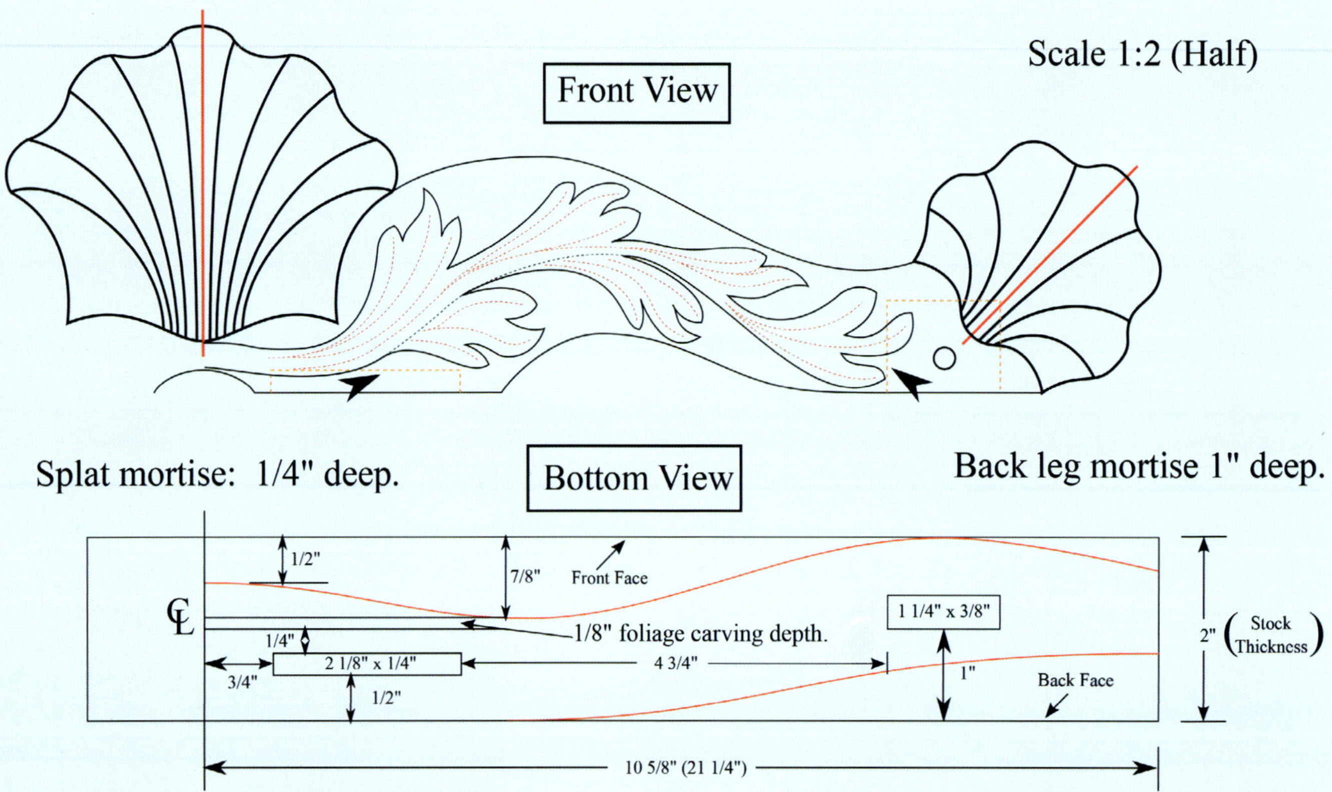

Figure 7-6. Half-scale drawing of the crest rail. This crest rail is cut from 8/4 stock 21 1/4" (l) x 4" (h). Square the bottom edge. Lay out and cut the mortises as described while the blank is square. After the mortises are cut, scale these templates to full size and draw them on the blank. Make sure they are more or less positioned as illustrated. Use a bandsaw to cut the bottom view first. Save the cut-away pieces and reattach with tape to restore the patterns. Use the bandsaw to cut the front view. The rough blank is now ready for transferring the carving template shapes.

This chapter describes how to carve ornamental embellishments on a crest rail that are typical of a Chippendale style chair. This particular example has three main elements and is found on the high end of chairs of this form. The reference model for this chair is in the Diplomatic Reception Rooms of the State Department. Figures 7-4 and 7-5 are my version of this chair and the crest rail, respectively.

Before any carved elements can be added, significant work goes into cutting and shaping the profile and background surface on which those elements will be carved. The shape of this crest rail requires two profiles; one is a bottom view and the other is the front view. Start with a piece of stock as described in figure 7-6. Using this same figure, make templates for both the front and bottom profiles and transfer them to the blank. Pay particular attention to the layout lines on the bottom edge beneath the central shell. Note that toward the front face there is ¼" left for the mortise wall and an additional ⅛" for the carved foliage. This line defines the depth of the central shell. (Note that I cut and fit all of my joints while the crest rail blank is square. When the joints fit, I then shape and carve the crest rail. This sequence makes cutting the mortises easier because the stock is square. In addition, I know that the rail will fit after it is carved.)

The first cut is along the bottom profile. Use a band saw for this operation. Save the waste pieces from these cuts and reattach them with some tape. These waste pieces are needed for the front profile and to provide a flat surface on the bottom. Use a band saw to cut along the front profile curves. Figure 7-7 shows the crest rail blank cut from the stock.

Carving Note: The red dashed lines in the foliage carving are center lines for various leaves. Use a 5mm, 9 gouge to scoop out along these center line. Switch to a wider one and follow the initial cuts. The ridges left by scooping cuts will be the separation lines between two adjacent leaves. When using the wider gouge, try to leave continuous ridge lines. This will give a nice shape and flow to the leaves. The green dashed line represents the ridge between the upper sprig of leaves and the two clusters below. The two clusters below are lower, so use a V-tool to cut along the line such that a smooth continuous curve connects the perimeter segments. Bevel into V cut from below.

Figure 7-7. The crest rail blank has just been cut from the stock.

CHIPPENDALE CHAIR CARVED CREST RAIL

As mentioned earlier, there are three unique carved elements on this crest rail: the central shell, the shell on each ear, and the acanthus in between. The strategy will be to separate and establish the surface shape for these elements before adding any detail. Start with the central shell. Make a template for this shell from the drawing in figure 7-6. Transfer the template to the blank as shown in figure 7-8. Set in straight down along the perimeter on the sides and bottom using a #5 12 mm gouge. Remove material down to the top of the carving layer line on the bottom edge as shown. Blend the cuts smoothly into the background surface. This will take a couple of iterations to get to the desired depth. The final depth should be about 5⁄16" from the highest spot at the center of the shell to the background surface at the shell perimeter. Figure 7-9 shows the shell established after reaching the desired depth.

Now work on one of the ear shells. First some shaping is needed. Make a mark ½" from the bottom surface on the edge of the center convex lobe of the ear shell. This mark will be used as the depth gauge for shaping the surface. Transfer the bottom edge of the ear shell template to the blank. Figure 7-10 shows the depth mark and shell edge. Use a #49 rasp to shape a smooth and uniform surface down to the depth line. At the same time, blend this surface into the background further back toward the center of the crest rail. Note that some of the template line may be removed. That's okay, it will be redrawn later. When the operation is complete, the view down the centerline of the ear shell should be such that the shell looks symmetric left to right around its centerline and falls off symmetrically and uniformly as the surface approaches the edge. While shaping the front surface of the ear, clean up the band saw marks on the edge. Define the curved sections better and blend them together. This doesn't have to be perfect at this point, just better than fresh off the band saw. Figure 7-11 shows the contoured surface with the bottom profile redrawn. Now the surface is ready for the ear shell.

Before the ear shell is raised, draw the other carved elements on the blank. This is necessary so that material that is needed for these elements won't be removed when raising the shell. Make a template for the foliage from the drawing in figure 7-6 and transfer it to the blank. Finally, this crest rail has an added detail of a button that is centered on the mortise. It is ¼" in diameter and its center is ½" up from the bottom. Figure 7-12 shows the layout complete.

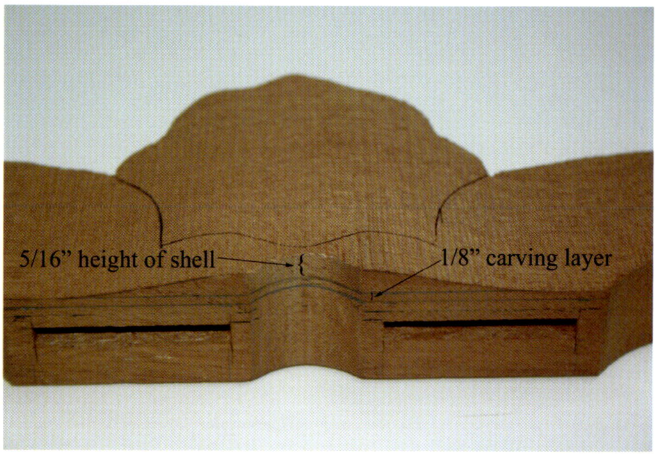

Figure 7-8. It's important to lay out the joints early, so that enough material can be left in the proper places to accommodate the various levels.

Figure 7-9. Set in along the shell perimeter and remove the material around it down to the top of the carving layer. Also blend the background into the surrounding surface.

Figure 7-10. The ear shell is ½" thick at its thinnest. Make the ½" mark on the edge.

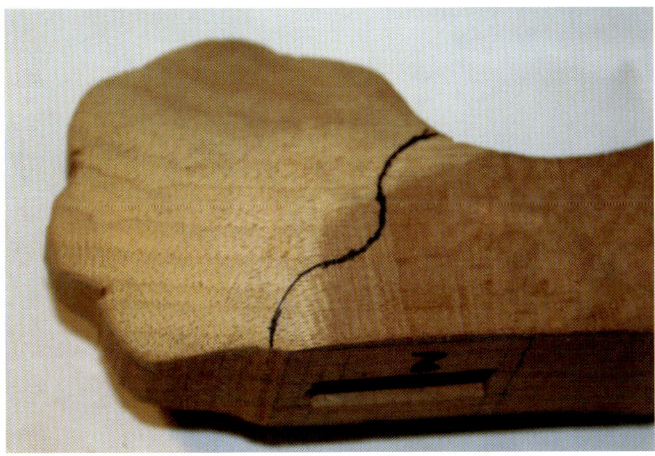

Figure 7-11. Rasp and file the ear shell to the depth mark. Strive for a smooth surface throughout and as it blends into the rest of the crest rail.

Figure 7-14. Clean up the background around the ear shell and its close neighbors.

Figure 7-12. Draw all of the elements so that they can be accommodated when raising any one of them.

Figure 7-13. Set in around the perimeters of the ear shell and the elements close to it. Bevel into the stop cuts, being careful not to impact any of the adjacent elements.

Figure 7-15. Draw the wings on the ear shell.

When doing a project of this complexity, judgment is needed every step along the way. These templates are as accurate as I can make them, but since no two iterations are the same, some tweaking may be needed. For example, when placing the foliage template, draw it in pieces. Make sure that portions are positioned correctly relative to other elements. There is a certain distance between the ear shell and the tip of the leaves. There is also a certain positioning of the leaves near the central shell. With these in place, move the template to connect these known portions together. In this way the template is made to "fit" the piece. The goal is that the foliage or any other element looks good in itself and relative to all the other elements. This technique allows one template to be "stretched" or "shrunk" to fit the circumstances of the specific piece. This should be one's mindset when doing any of this type work. These are not manufactured and interchangeable parts. Each one is slightly different, so slight modifications are frequently needed. Once this concept is fully appreciated, it is liberating because mistakes can be corrected without starting over and dimensions become guidelines and not rigid absolutes.

Back to the ear shell. Set in along the lower edge with a #5 8 mm gouge and bevel into this cut from the outside. This will "raise" the ear shell from the background. Set in and cut around the button and the tips of the leaves when beveling into the shell line. A #7 6 mm gouge works well for the button. Appropriately sized #5 and #7 gouges match the leaf tips. Figure 7-13 shows early progress and figure 7-14 shows the ear shell, button, and leaf tips raised from the background.

Continue with the ear shell by transferring the lines from the template as shown in figure 7-15. Use a #5 8 mm gouge to set in along these lines and bevel into them as shown in figure 7-16. Be careful around the root to avoid breakage. This step separates the "wings" from the "lobes" of the shell. Around the root you may have to lower the background a little to accommodate the extra level of the wings. If so, remove a little of the background and blend it into the surrounding area. This is a common procedure with these elements and it is all part of the process.

Figure 7-16. Set in along the wing lines and bevel into the stop cut. Blend the wing surface into the base of the stop cut, keeping the outer perimeter high.

Figure 7-17. Freehand draw the centerlines for each of the concave lobes. Split the root into evenly spaced segments and connect each one with the center of the concave lobe.

Figure 7-18. Use a #9 13 mm gouge to cut a trough along the centerlines.

Figure 7-19. Use a flat chisel to round over the edges of the gouge cuts to form the convex lobes.

Figure 7-22. Round the shell down to the ⅝" mark while leaving the dot on the surface high.

Figure 7-20. Blend the concave and convex lobes into a smooth, continuous, undulating surface. Use files and rounded scrapers for the final blending.

Figure 7-23. Use a #49 rasp to begin shaping the shell.

Figure 7-21. Raise the foliage. Set in around the perimeter and level the background into the stop cuts.

Next freehand the lines shown in figure 7-17. These lines represent the centers of the concave lobes. Evenly space them at the root and fan them out to the center of the inward depressions at the perimeter. This shell is going to be a smooth, continuous, alternating sequence of convex and concave lobes; there are no ridges or steps. Use a #9 13 mm gouge to carve along the lines just drawn as shown in figure 7-18. Be aggressive with the depth, especially at the perimeter. Use a flat chisel to round over the edges formed by the gouge cuts. This will start to define the convex lobes as well as give better access for deepening the concave ones. Switch to narrower #9 or #11 gouges when carving into the root. Figure 7-19 shows late progress toward roughing the shape. Blend all facets and irregularities using scrapers, files, and sandpaper. Rounded scrapers of various radii work very well here. Figure 7-20 shows the completed shape.

Now "raise" the foliage. Start by setting in along the perimeter with appropriately shaped gouges and beveling into these stop cuts. A variety of carving gouges will be needed to match the curves of the drawing. Typically #7 6 mm and #7 10 mm gouges will give nice leaf tips and #5 8 mm and #3 8 mm ones will transition between leaves. This is not absolute, so use the drawing and the tools available to guide you. Let the tools determine the final shape if they don't match the drawing perfectly. In this way the curves will blend much nicer and the forms will be pleasing to the eye, which is the goal. Bevel into the stop cuts with small-width #2 and #3 gouges. Note that the central shell will get a little deeper as the leaves near it are raised. Removing this background is a little more tedious because of the tight spaces. Small, flat chisels with the bevel down work well as do small, flat skew chisels. When the background surfaces are close, but rough, I use small, bent rifflers to smooth them out. Figure 7-21 shows the foliage fully raised.

The central shell is isolated, but not fully shaped. Make the two marks as shown in figure 7-22. The point on the surface of the shell will remain high and the surface will fall off from it in all directions. The mark on the top edge of the central shell is ⅝" up from the bottom along the centerline. This is the depth of the surface at the top. Use a #49 rasp to shape the shell surface. Leave the tips of the outer lobes about ⅛" above the background and the lower root about 1⁄16" above the foliage envelope. Figure 7-23 shows intermediate progress and figure 7-24 shows the operation complete. Note the relative heights of the various levels.

Start the central shell by drawing the guide marks shown in figure 7-25. Make tick marks in the root and at the outside perimeter and then connect corresponding ones with a smooth curve. Use the template to position the perimeter marks and draw the wing lines. In the root, position a ruler so that there is a mark on each of the wing lines and there are eight marks between them. Draw a tick at each of the eight ruler marks.

With a pencil, connect the endpoints of each ray line freehand. Position your hand so that the anchored portion can be used as a pivot. For some, the ray can be drawn in one sweep. For others, draw a little from each end and then move your hand and connect the segments. Figure 7-26 shows the lines in place. Note that the foliage on both sides of the central shell have been excavated. This is needed so there is better access to the shell elements.

Establish the side wings first. Use a #5 12 mm gouge to set in perpendicular to the surface along the outer ray line as shown in figure 7-27. Remove all of the material on the outside of this line to the edge of the shell envelope. The goal is to have a flat surface that is about 1⁄16" high. This will take a few iterations to get to the proper depth. Figure 7-28 shows the operation complete. Now do the same thing on the other side.

The remainder of the carving is to establish alternating convex and concave lobes. There are nine lobes total with five convex and four concave. Separate two adjacent lobes using a V-tool. Start somewhere in the middle of a ray line and work toward each end. The grain will determine which direction the cuts should go. Make very shallow cuts to start. This will minimize tear-out and help establish a nice curved line. Figure 7-29 shows early progress. Be particularly careful near both ends because there is a lot of short grain that can easily chip out. A technique that helps here is to cut straight down on the line with a flatter gouge and bevel into this line from either side. The goal is to have a V channel running the length of the ray line. Round over the edge on the convex side using a ½" flat chisel. Keep the walls of the concave lobes at an angle. This will give much better support to the lobe and avoid breakages when the lobe is scooped out later. Figure 7-30 shows intermediate progress.

Figure 7-24. Use a file to get a smooth surface. The surface falls off in all directions from the high point.

Figure 7-27. Set in along the wing line with a #5 12 mm gouge.

Figure 7-25. Position a ruler so that there is a mark on each wing line and eight marks in between. Draw a tick at each of the interior marks. The ticks on the outer perimeter are the lobe boundaries. Use the template to position these.

Figure 7-28. Lower the wing to about $\frac{1}{16}$".

Figure 7-26. Connect corresponding ticks freehand using your hand as a pivot.

Figure 7-29. Use a V-tool to define the lobe boundaries.

Repeat this process on the other side of the concave lobe. Figure 7-31 shows two convex lobes with an area for a concave lobe between them.

Scoop out the center of the concave lobe using a series of #9 gouges. Use wider ones toward the outer edge and narrower ones toward the root. Figure 7-32 shows the initial concave cut. Extend the trough side to side to the wall edges and taper it as the lobe narrows. Because the width of each lobe is very narrow at the root, don't scoop out the center in this area. Taper the trough from a point where it becomes too narrow to safely make the concave cut, and slightly round over the edges in this area even for the concave lobes. This means that all of the lobes in the root area will have a slight convex curvature. Repeat the process for the remaining lobes. Figure 7-33 shows all of the lobes complete.

Use the foliage template from figure 7-6 as a guide to draw the perimeter lines that define the individual leaves. Sketch these by hand and strive for smoothness and flow. Figure 7-34 shows these lines drawn on the foliage blank.

The goal is to scoop out each leaf between the defining perimeter lines, leaving the lines high. This will make the layout lines ridges, which will visually define each leaf. So these ridge lines need to be carved as nice, flowing curves without unsightly irregularities. Start with the lower cluster as shown in figure 7-35. Use a #9 7 mm gouge to scoop the center of each leaf. Switch to a narrower #9 as the width requires.

Move to the cluster just above this one and separate the leaves in the same manner. Figure 7-36 shows the center troughs and how they flow together. A series of #9 gouges are used for the vast majority of the troughs. Figure 7-37 shows the next cluster brought to the same level of refinement.

Use a #11 2 mm gouge to cut along the line shown in figure 7-38. This will separate the three leaf clusters to the right from the ones closer to the center. It also allows the bottom line of the upper section to flow unbroken to its tip. This is a subtle distinction, but it all adds to the illusion of leaves hanging on the chair.

Separate each of the leaves in their respective clusters in the same manner as previously done. Figure 7-39 shows three groups done. The foliage on the other side of the central shell is a mirror image of this. Repeat the same steps on that section.

Figure 7-30. Complete the lobe separation with the V-tool. Round the convex lobes using a flat chisel.

Figure 7-31. More progress on the convex lobes. Blend the facets with a file.

Figure 7-32. Scoop the concave lobes using #9 gouges. Start at the perimeter.

Figure 7-33. All of the lobes are convex in the narrow root area.

Figure 7-34. Draw freehand lines to separate the leaves.

Figure 7-35. Scoop each leaf, leaving the ridge between adjacent ones as the dividing line.

Figure 7-36. One stem branches into two leaves with a third between.

Figure 7-37. Three clusters complete.

Figure 7-38. Use a #11 5 mm gouge to separate the lower cluster.

Figure 7-39. Define each of the leaves in a similar manner.

At this point, all that remains is to add some detail lines to the various elements. The ear shells have a hatched pattern as shown in figure 7-40. Draw the lines first, so that if you need to make any adjustment it is easy to correct. The number of lines is not critical, so position them so they look good on your surface. Also be careful on the narrow portion of the convex lobes; there is not much room, so it is better to not have a hatch line than to have one so small that the wood breaks. It will work best to start each leg of a "V" at its vertex when carving. Use a #11 1 mm gouge to carve these lines.

The central shell wings have detail lines as shown in figure 7-41. And each of the leaves have veins added as shown in figure 7-42. Use a #11 1 mm gouge for these also.

The crest rail is now complete and is ready to be added to your chair.

Figure 7-40. Draw the V-lines on the ear shell and carve them with a #11 1 mm gouge.

Figure 7-41. Draw the detail lines on the wings and carve them with a #11 1 mm gouge.

Figure 7-42. Use the #11 1 mm gouge to cut some veins in each of the leaves.

PHILADELPHIA CHIPPENDALE CHAIR PIERCED AND CARVED BACK SPLAT

The back splat is one of the major focal points of an eighteenth-century Philadelphia chair. In the earlier Queen Anne style, there was little if any carved embellishment. The crest rail, splat, and back legs worked together to form a bird's beak in the negative space. In this case the shape and form were the ornamentation. In the later Chippendale style, the bird's beak went away and carved embellishments were added for ornamentation.

Figure 8-1.

Figure 8-2.

Figure 8-3.

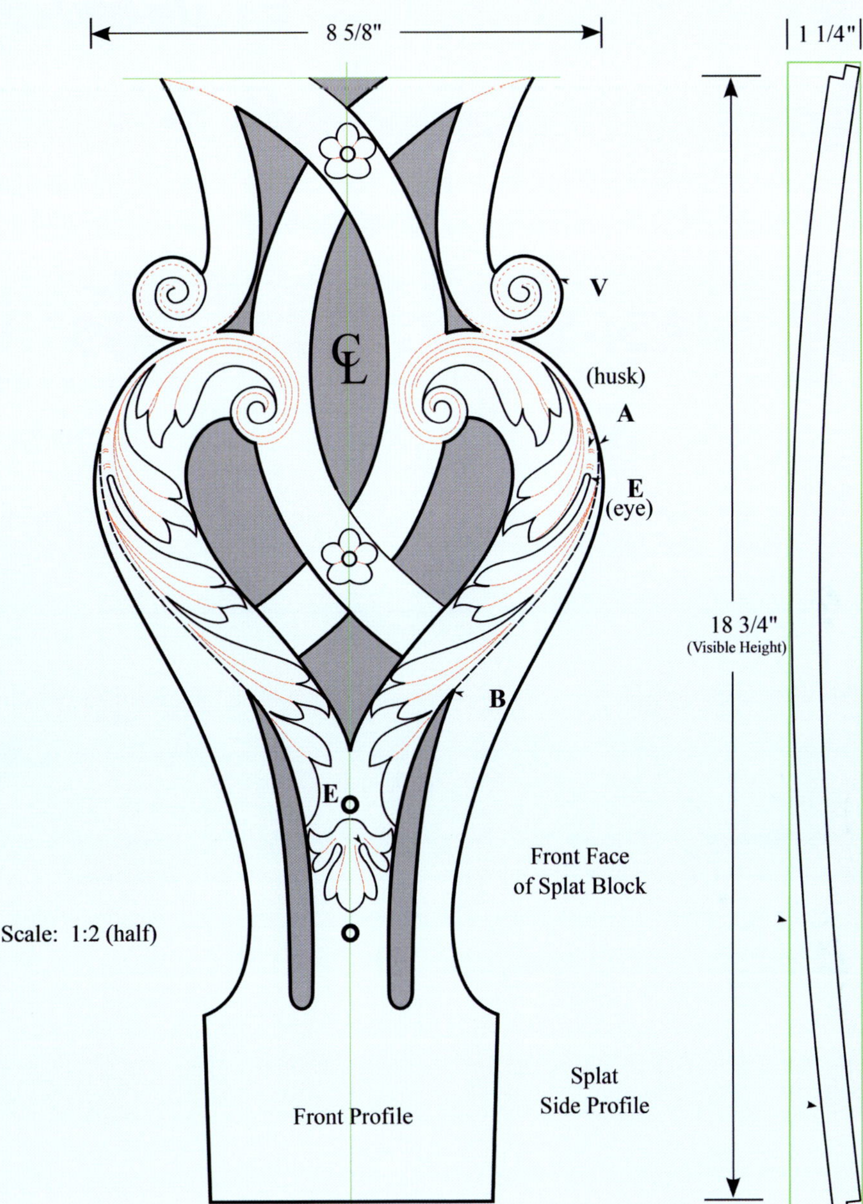

Figure 8-4. needs to be added to the top and bottom of the Front Profile to account for the tenon on each end.

At the same time the splat became more visibly delicate with portions removed that allowed for an overlapping ribbon motif. On the higher-style chairs, carved foliage, scrolls, and other elements were added to enhance the appearance. Figures 8-1 through 8-3 show three examples of high-style carved splats.

The back splat that I describe here is taken from the same high-end State Department side chair as the crest rail from the previous chapter.

To stay focused on carving, I am going to skip the steps to prepare the splat. For a highlighted version of how to cut the splat from the blank and prepare it for carving, see the Splat Preparation Inset section at the end of this chapter. I cut the joints and fit the splat into the chair back before carving. This has two purposes. First, it is easier to cut the joints before the splat is carved because the reference surfaces are better. Second, if needed, I can make adjustments to the template placement relative to square. Since the scope of this chapter is the carving, I am not going to further discuss how to fit the splat.

Now that the splat blank is ready for carving, some thoughts about a strategy. The first thing to note about this splat is that there are three different levels. Study the picture of a completed version in figure 8-3 and the line drawing in figure 8-4 to understand how the different levels interact. Also note how the ribbons overlap. At the top, the right-hand ribbon overlaps the left and tucks underneath it farther down.

CHIPPENDALE CHAIR PIERCED AND CARVED BACK SPLAT

Draw a centerline on the convex side of the blank. Now make a full-scale template of one-half of the front profile from figure 8-4 and transfer it. Figure 8-5 shows the template transferred to the blank. Drill a 3/16" hole in each of the interior sections as shown in figure 8-6. Cut these out with a scroll saw. Figure 8-7 shows the results. Use a band saw to cut the outside profile. The scroll saw would work here, but I prefer the band saw because it is quicker and I can make the cut more accurate. Figure 8-8 shows the splat completely cut from the blank. Note the areas labeled "A." Leave extra material here so that it can be blended into the crest rail after assembly. This is also a good time to clean up the saw cuts and bevel those cuts toward the back face.

Start the carving by "raising" the two flowers on the centerline of the splat. Set in around the perimeter with a #7 6 mm gouge and bevel into these stop cuts with a #5 5 mm gouge. The depth should be no more than 1/16". Figure 8-9 shows the flower raised. Feather the background around each flower so that the surface is smooth and uniform. Remove the minimal amount of material from the background as is necessary. The goal is to create a look that the flower is sitting on top of the background surface. Some of the ribbon boundary lines may be removed in this operation. That is okay; they will be redrawn later. Figure 8-10 shows the background smoothed.

In a similar manner, set in around the volute and foliage area that overlays the ribbon strands and bevel back into these cuts. Blend the background surface into these cuts as was done for the flowers. Figure 8-11 shows the volute raised and the background smoothed and blended.

Now raise the foliage as shown in figure 8-12. Note how the outside line of the foliage envelope gracefully connects the shoulder curve at the top with the inside curve of the cutout at the bottom. These are labeled "A" and "B" in figure 8-4. It's important to keep this curve graceful as you raise the foliage, because your eye will be able to easily pick up any irregularities. Use a #3 12 mm gouge to set in at the top. Position the gouge so that part of the cutting edge is off the blank and part of it is on it. At the same time, keep the part that is off the blank tight to the outside curve of the blank. This will give a smooth transition from the outside curve to the curve on the blank surface. Figure 8-13 shows the technique. In a similar manner, use a #2 12 mm gouge at the point labeled "B." With the #2 gouge, bevel into the stop cut and blend into the background to form a smooth, uniform surface. Figure 8-14 shows the result.

Figure 8-5. Transfer the splat template to the cleaned-up blank. The pattern needs to be square to the mortise shoulder at the top.

Figure 8-6. Drill access holes in the interior cutout sections.

Figure 8-7. Use a scroll saw to cut out the interior sections.

Figure 8-8. Use a band saw or scroll saw to cut the exterior.

Figure 8-9. Raise the flower by setting in along its perimeter and beveling into the stop cut.

Figure 8-10. Blend the background around the flower so that it is smooth to the eye and touch.

Figure 8-11. Raise the volute in a similar manner.

CHIPPENDALE CHAIR PIERCED AND CARVED BACK SPLAT

Next raise the inside edges of the foliage and the other elements on the central portion. Use a variety of #2, #3, #5, and #7 gouges as needed to match the various curves. A #11 2 mm gouge is appropriate for the "eyes" labeled "E" in figure 8-4. Figure 8-15 shows intermediate progress and figure 8-16 shows this step completed. Use rifflers to clean up the background, especially in the tight areas between leaves.

Separate the volute labeled "V" in figure 8-4 from the foliage below it. Note that the volute is on top, so that is the curve to set in on. Use a #7 6 mm gouge at the center and finish with a #3 12 mm gouge to connect the outside curve of the volute with the outer edge of the blank.

Next establish the volute by first drawing a guideline as shown in figure 8-17. Use the template to position this curve correctly. This line represents the high point of the bevel that will raise the spiral. Draw the additional curve shown in figure 8-18. This curve represents the extent of the bevel. Use a #7 6 mm gouge near the center to bevel into the stop cut. Figure 8-19 shows the progress. Try to get a nice, crisp point at the intersection of the bevel and the innermost point of the volute. A technique for blending the beveled background is to overlap successive cuts and move the gouge in a slicing motion into the stop cut. Switch to a #5 or a #3 8 mm gouge to blend the facets left by the #7. Figure 8-20 shows this step complete.

Finally, separate the central ribbon strands. Note which ribbon is on top at the intersection areas. Use the template from figure 8-4 to redraw the ribbon edge curves. Figure 8-21 shows the ribbon lines in place. Next set in along these lines with a #2 12 mm gouge. Bevel into the stop cuts with the same gouge. Figure 8-22 shows the ribbons separated. Smooth and blend the background as in previous steps. At this point all of the levels are established and the element envelopes are raised. What remains is to detail each element.

Start with the volute and foliage. Study the red detail lines in figure 8-4 and the completed splat in figure 8-3 to understand how to separate the leaves. For the most part, the red lines are ridge lines formed by scooping out the center of the leaves on either side. Keep this in mind while making the various cuts. I will describe the right-hand portion so any references are relative to that one.

Establish the volute first. Use the same techniques and gouges as for the one carved earlier. Carve the bevel as shown in figure 8-23. Leave the background high immediately after clearing the volute. The foliage will emanate from the background in this area, so don't remove too much too soon.

Figure 8-12. Raise the foliage envelope.

Figure 8-13. The foliage blends into the perimeter of the blank. Use a #3 12 mm gouge to make the transition.

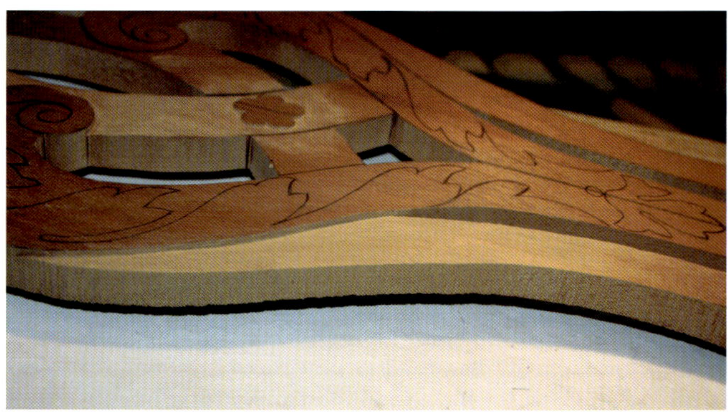

Figure 8-14. Blend the background to a smooth surface.

Figure 8-15. Raise the leaf tips.

Figure 8-16. The entire foliage envelope is raised above the background.

Figure 8-17. Use the template to draw the volute perimeter.

Figure 8-18. Draw a guide line to define the extent of the bevel.

Figure 8-19. Set in along the volute line and bevel into the stop cut. Extend the bevel to the guide line.

Figure 8-20. Blend and feather the background to a smooth, gentle ramp.

Next define the husk that straddles the "eye" connecting the second and third leaf clusters. Draw the lines shown in figure 8-24. Use a #9 3 mm gouge to define the husk as shown in figure 8-25. Note that this cut connects back to the background of the volute. Note that this cut also separates the top leaf cluster from the one just below it.

Use the #9 10 mm gouge to scoop out the centers of each of the leaves in the upper two clusters. The technique that works for me is to use a larger gouge at the tips first and then use a smaller gouge at the root and blend into each leaf. As the troughs converge to a common root farther away from the leaf tips, switch to a narrower #9 or #11 if things get too tight. Another way to think of it is that each cluster begins at a common point and the troughs diverge from there into the separate leaf tips. Figures 8-26 and 8-27 show different stages of progress. The ridge lines should form smooth curves as they define the boundaries between adjacent leaves.

Now establish the lower side of the husk. The husk is on the perimeter of the blank at the shoulder, and the trough that defines its extension as it comes back onto the foliage envelope goes down the center of the leaf just below the husk. Use a small, flat chisel to round over the edges of the husk. The goal is to make the husk a cornucopia. Figure 8-28 shows the shaped husk. Detail the leaves in this lower cluster in the same way as before. Figure 8-29 shows the lower cluster.

Note that there are three pairs of arcs on the surface of the husk. These are cut with a #7 4 mm gouge. With the bevel of the gouge up, cut at an angle a little greater than straight down. This is the opposite of undercutting and forms the arc. Now with the bevel up, cut into this arc. These are shallow, delicate cuts, so use light pressure and short strokes. The location of these arcs is not critical. The goal is to have two close together and some visible distance between the pairs. As the husk narrows, the arcs get smaller and more delicate. These arcs give the sense of curvature and bend to the husk, which is a realistic effect. Figure 8-30 shows the three pairs complete.

Move to the bottom leaf cluster next. As before, the detail lines in the drawing in figure 8-4 are ridge lines formed by adjacent troughs merging. Draw in the leaf separation lines as shown in figure 8-31. Use a #9 10 mm gouge to scoop each leaf. Start in the wide part of the leaf and blend the troughs as they converge. Now round over the edges of the root, keeping its center high. Blend the convex surface from the root into the concave surfaces from the leaves. Finally, round over the buttons on top and bottom. Figure 8-32 shows the

Figure 8-21. Determine which ribbon is on top and draw the boundary. In this case the left one is on top in this area.

Figure 8-22. Set in along the boundary lines and bevel into the stop cuts on the ribbon underneath.

Figure 8-23. Raise the volute on this ribbon.

Figure 8-24. Define the "husk" that straddles the "eye." Note that each leg of the husk branches into its own leaf cluster.

Figure 8-25. Use a #11 2 mm gouge to establish each side of the husk.

Figure 8-26. Scoop each leaf so that the ridges between the gouge cuts conform to the lines that define each one. Each cluster starts from a common point and branches out.

Figure 8-27. Define the leaves in the next cluster in a similar manner.

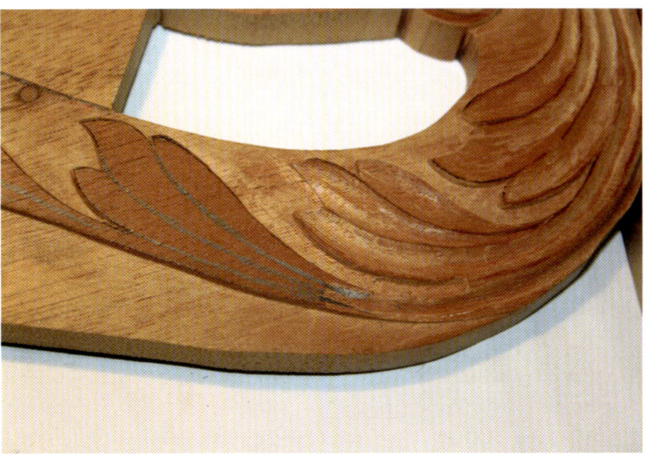

Figure 8-28. Round over the husk to form a cornucopia.

completed element. Use a #11 1 mm gouge to make detail lines as shown in the completed splat in figure 8-3.

Next work on one of the flowers on the ribbons. Draw in the lines as shown in figure 8-33. Isolate the central button by setting in around the perimeter with a #7 6 mm gouge. Raise the button by beveling into the stop cut. Figure 8-34 shows the result. Next use a #9 7 mm gouge to scoop each leaf. Go deep enough to give nice definition to each leaf. The ridges formed by two adjacent trough cuts are the dividing lines between two petals. Figure 8-35 show the leaves separated and scooped. When each petal is sufficiently defined, use a #11 1 mm gouge to add radial accent lines. Round over the top of the central button by beveling the outer edge and smoothing the surface. Figure 8-36 shows the completed flower.

The splat is now complete and ready to be installed in the chair back.

Splat Preparation Inset

This back splat is cut from a 5/4-thick piece of stock. If multiple chairs are being made, spoon two or more splats together to conserve wood. Two splats can be gotten from an 8/4 board, etc. Start by transferring the side profile to the side of the blank. Allow extra length at each end for the ¼" tenons, both top and bottom. Use a band saw to cut along both the side profile lines. It is good to square the edges of the blank so that there is a smooth, flat surface on the band saw table. It also makes drawing the profile easier and more accurate.

These cuts are a little tricky because of the height of blank. It is easy for the blade to drift so that the cut on the visible top is good but the one at the hidden bottom is too thin. To help with this, use a sharp saw blade and a fence with a line contact extension if possible. The sharp blade will tend to drift less and the line contact fence will give you a visual and physical reference at the bottom.

After the blank has been cut from the stock, a lot of smoothing and cleanup is needed. Use a block plane across the grain or skewed to it on the convex side. This will remove wood quickly. Then use rasps, files, scrapers, and sandpaper to create a smooth and uniform surface. The plane will not work well on the concave side, but the other smoothing tools work fine. Get this surface as good as possible at this point, because it will be harder later if you have to do more significant smoothing. To see where more cleanup is needed, sight the blank from a low angle. This view will clearly show any irregularities.

Figure 8-29. Shape the leaves in the cluster below the husk.

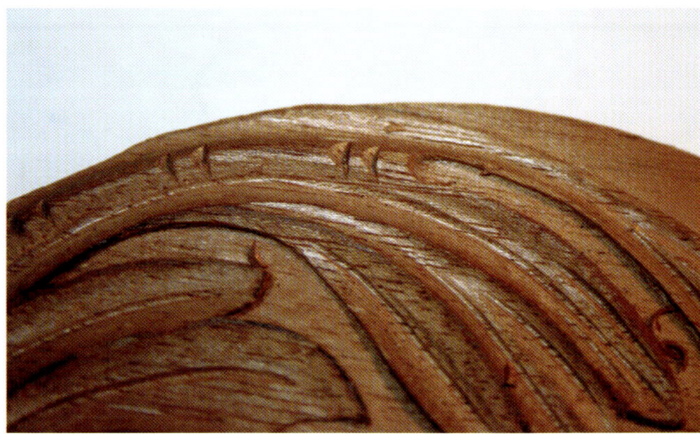

Figure 8-30. Make small pairs of cut marks along the line of the cornucopia. Two cuts should be close together with some separation between the pairs.

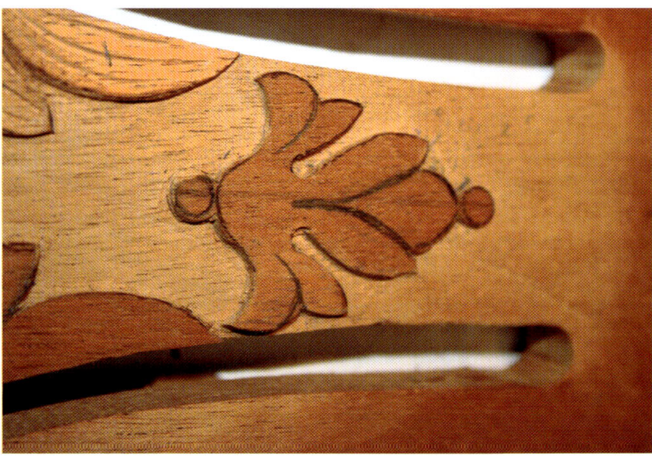

Figure 8-31. Raise the leaf cluster at the bottom of the splat and draw the leaf separation lines.

Figure 8-32. Scoop the individual leaves with the ridges following the leaf separation lines.

Figure 8-35. Use a #9 7 mm gouge to scoop each leaf.

Figure 8-33. To shape the flower, separate it into five leaves with a center dome.

Figure 8-36. Add some veins to each leaf with a #11 1 mm gouge.

Figure 8-34. Set in around the center with a #7 6 mm gouge and bevel into the stop cut.

JOHN GODDARD OPEN TALON BALL AND CLAW FOOT

The open talon ball and claw foot is one of the most recognized and iconic forms of eighteenth-century American furniture. It was exclusively made by members of the Townsend and Goddard families in Newport, Rhode Island, in the last quarter of that century. Newport was one of the four major design centers of the day, the other three being Philadelphia, Boston, and New York. None of the other regional centers produced an open talon foot; however, they did have their own unique characteristics. Although the Townsend and Goddard families were connected through marriage, they produced two distinct variations of an open talon foot. One is associated with John Goddard and the other with John Townsend.

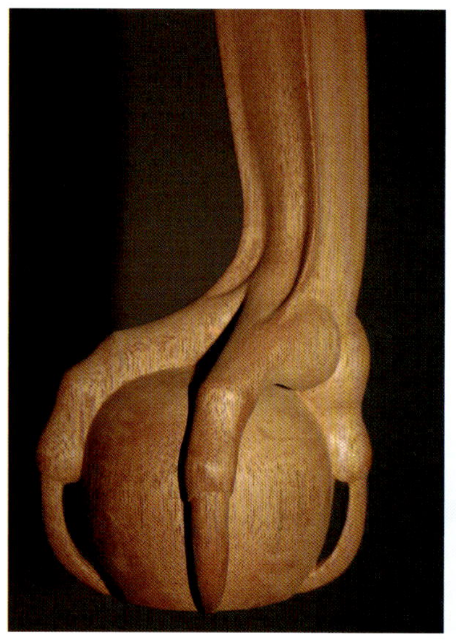

Figure 9-1. The completed foot. Refer to it for details as you progress through the steps. *Table photo by Ramon Moreno.*

The Townsend foot is stylistically simpler and characterized by tall toes with a lot of tension. The talons are open, but the top of the ball is not. The Goddard foot, shown in figure 9-1, has distinctive ankle bones on the side toes and a bulbous top knuckle on the back toe. The talons are open, as is the top of the ball. These openings give a dramatic and delicate look that is unique. It is the Goddard foot that I will describe in this chapter.

I have adapted the engineering method that I described in my first book to this foot. Extracting the ball is identical to the Philadelphia foot and shaping the lower portion of the toes is very similar. The differences are in the upper portions of the toes where they transition to the ankle, and the openings in the talons and the top of the ball.

The foot that I describe here is for a tea table, although the same size foot is found on Newport high chests, too. To get started, shape a cabriole leg from a 3" × 3" blank of necessary height. I am not going to describe shaping the leg since that is not the purpose of the chapter. One thing to note about a Newport cabriole leg is that the corners are much sharper than they are on a Philadelphia leg.

JOHN GODDARD OPEN TALON BALL AND CLAW FOOR LAYOUT

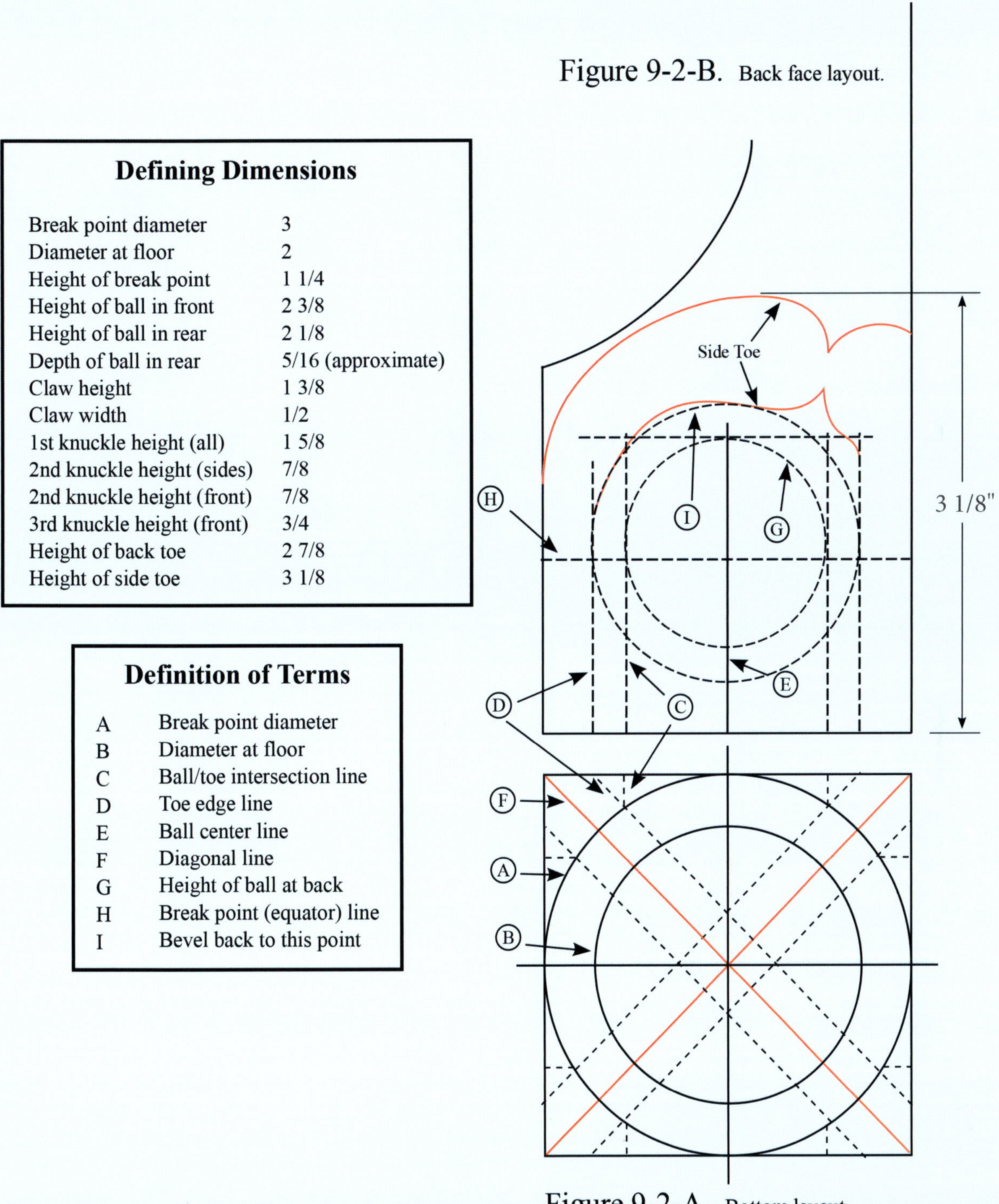

Defining Dimensions

Break point diameter	3
Diameter at floor	2
Height of break point	1 1/4
Height of ball in front	2 3/8
Height of ball in rear	2 1/8
Depth of ball in rear	5/16 (approximate)
Claw height	1 3/8
Claw width	1/2
1st knuckle height (all)	1 5/8
2nd knuckle height (sides)	7/8
2nd knuckle height (front)	7/8
3rd knuckle height (front)	3/4
Height of back toe	2 7/8
Height of side toe	3 1/8

Definition of Terms

A	Break point diameter
B	Diameter at floor
C	Ball/toe intersection line
D	Toe edge line
E	Ball center line
F	Diagonal line
G	Height of ball at back
H	Break point (equator) line
I	Bevel back to this point

Figure 9-2-B. Back face layout.

Figure 9-2-A. Bottom layout.

Figure 9-2. These diagrams show the layout and defining dimensions for the Goddard foot.

OPEN TALON BALL AND CLAW FOOT

After the cabriole shape has been cut and smoothed, transfer the layout from figure 9-2-A to the bottom of the foot. The inner circle is the diameter of the ball at the floor and the outer circle is the diameter of the ball at the "break point." The "break point" is the widest part of the ball, and is 1¼" from the floor. I use a divider to scribe the inner circle and then trace it with a 0.5 mm mechanical pencil. In this way there will be a nice, crisp line when carving the ball to it, and the pencil line makes it easier to see.

Extend the lines up the vertical faces of the blank as shown in figure 9-3. These will be used as further layout and guide lines for sawing out the toes. In addition, use a square to draw the "break point" line around the entire perimeter of the blank. Recall that the line is 1¼" from the bottom.

Next draw the elements shown in figure 9-2-B on each of the back faces. Make a template from the drawing labeled "Side Toe" in figure 9-2-B and transfer it to the two back faces of the blank as shown in figure 9-4. The highest point of the side toe is 3⅛" from the bottom. This template establishes the size, position, and spatial relationships between the side toes, the back toe, and the transition from the back face to the front face. Next use a compass to draw the two semi-circles, also shown in 9-4. At its highest point the inner arc is 2" from the bottom and outer one is 2⅜". Set the compass to be the distance between the vertical centerline and one of the "ball/toe intersection lines" as shown in figure 9-5. With this distance, center the compass on the vertical centerline so that the drawing point hits the 2" mark at the center. Draw the semi-circular arc to connect the two inner vertical lines labeled "A" shown in figure 9-5. This arc may not be centered exactly at the center of the ball. That is okay since these lines are to help approximate the ball and any slight variation is within the range of acceptability. Use the same compass center point and draw a larger semi-circle connecting the outer lines labeled "B" shown in figure 9-5.

The next step is to saw along the toe edges. The cuts on the front faces go down the entire depth to the outer circle. The ones on the back faces need to be cut at an angle to the outer circle depth at the foot bottom inclined to the "break point" line. If the cut goes higher than this it will impact the back and side toes. Figure 9-6 shows these cuts on both a front and a back face.

The first goal is to shape the ball, leaving the material needed for the toes intact. This translates into creating four separate sections of the ball that visually look like one surface. The two back faces are the same, but different from the two front faces, which are also the same. The strategy to creating the ball from a cube is to first turn the cube into a circular cylinder, and then round the top and bottom of the cylinder to form a sphere. Since each face is separate and independent, it is an arbitrary decision where to start. I usually start with one of the back faces for no particular reason.

On the back face, the top of the ball needs to be established while at the same time the toes are isolated. Set in vertically along the smaller arc using a #5 12 mm gouge. Figure 9-7 shows the technique. With the same tool, bevel into this stop cut from above, staying below the outer arc. The goal is to carve a bevel from the outer arc and its vertical lines down to the inner arc and its vertical lines to the depth of the outer circle as drawn on the bottom. This is done iteratively by setting in along the inner arc and vertical lines and beveling from the outer ones. Blend the curved bevel into the saw cut along the edges of the toes. Figures 9-8 and 9-9 show early and intermediate progress and figure 9-10 shows the operation complete. A #7 16 mm gouge will work well for carving the bevel along the tighter curves and a flat chisel works for the straight portions. Use a #5 12 mm gouge to blend the transitions between the flat and curved parts.

Now form a cylindrical section by rounding the isolated portion just carved to the outer circle on the bottom. Use a ½" flat chisel for this operation. This step doesn't have to be perfect since most of the cylindrical surface will be removed in the next step. The idea is to get a decent curve side to side that follows the outer circle. Be careful near the top so that the corner of the chisel doesn't catch in the circular bevel. A few shallow nicks are inevitable, but try to avoid deep ones. These could be difficult to remove later. Figure 9-11 shows the operation complete.

Next redraw the "break point" line. Make a couple of marks 1¼" from the bottom on the curved surface and connect them, using your finger as a fence. Now round over the top and bottom sections leaving the "break point" line intact. On the top, round down to the intersection with the beveled surface. On the bottom, round down to the inner circle. Avoid undercutting the toes on the bottom section. To do this, use a flat chisel with the back flush to the exposed toe surface and cut at an angle into the cylinder at the bottom. Figure 9-12 shows the technique. With the same flat chisel, cut off the bottom edge into the toe. Figure 9-13 shows the result. As the cuts at the bottom near the inner circle, blend further up toward the "break point" line. Figures 9-14, 9-15, and 9-16 show early, intermediate, and late progress, respectively. To help with forming a spherical surface, a #3 25 mm gouge matches the surface pretty well. I like to use a flat chisel to get a close approximation and then the #3 to refine the shape and remove the high spots. In this way I am much less likely to catch a corner of the gouge on the ball surface. After the ball has been carved, remove the remaining facets with a small, flat file. Move the file continuously, blending the facets and keeping an eye for a smooth and uniform spherical surface. As a last step, I use a small piece of 120-grit sandpaper and my finger to remove the file marks. Figure 9-17 shows the file technique and figure 9-18 shows this section of the ball complete. Repeat these steps to complete the other back face section.

Figure 9-3. Extend the layout lines up the face of the blank.

Figure 9-4. Transfer the side toe profile. This helps to position the ball and keep all of the layout consistent.

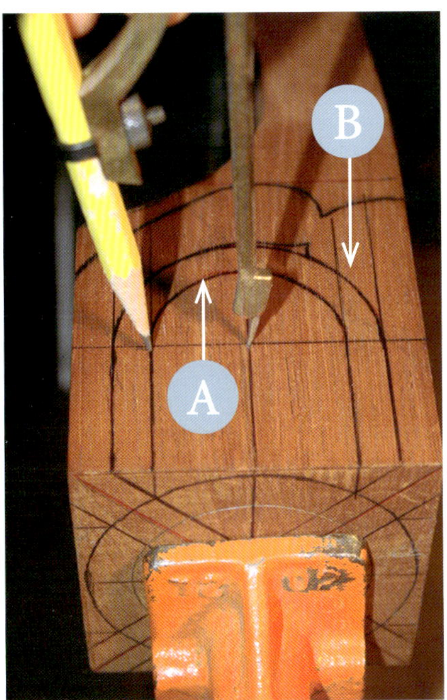

Figure 9-5. Use a compass to draw the ball profile.

Figure 9-6. Use a hand saw to cut along the edges of the toe. On the back edge of the side toes, the cut must stop at the break point. If it goes higher, the side toe will be ruined.

Figure 9-7. Excavate the top of the ball in back. Use a #5 12 mm gouge to set in along the inner semi-circle and bevel into this cut to the outside semi-circle.

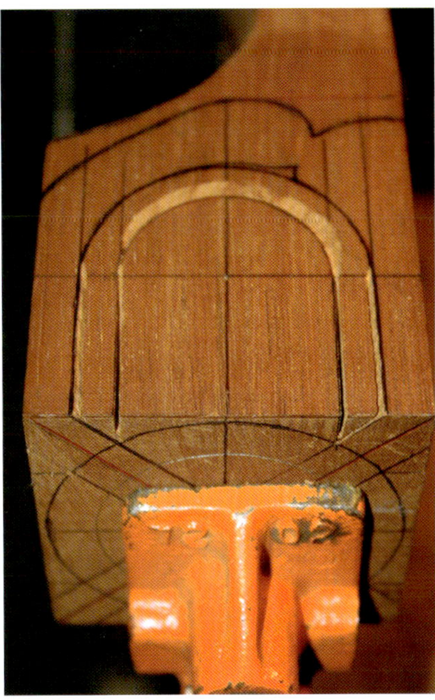

Figure 9-8. Bevel back into the top cut.

Figure 9-9. Blend the surface between the semi-circles to those delineated by the toe sides.

Figure 9-10. The back section of the ball is isolated.

Figure 9-12. Avoid undercutting the toes by using the toe side as guide and reference surface.

Figure 9-14. Round the top edge with a flat chisel.

Figure 9-11. Form a cylinder by carving to the outside circle on the foot bottom. Redraw the break point line after the cylinder is cut.

Figure 9-13. Use a flat chisel to remove the bottom corner of the cylinder.

Figure 9-15. More progress turning the cylinder into a sphere.

Figure 9-16. After the sphere is approximated with the flat chisel, use a #3 20 mm gouge to blend the facets and help form a spherical section.

Figure 9-18. This section of the ball is complete. This is one-quarter of the ball and it is formed and separated from the toes.

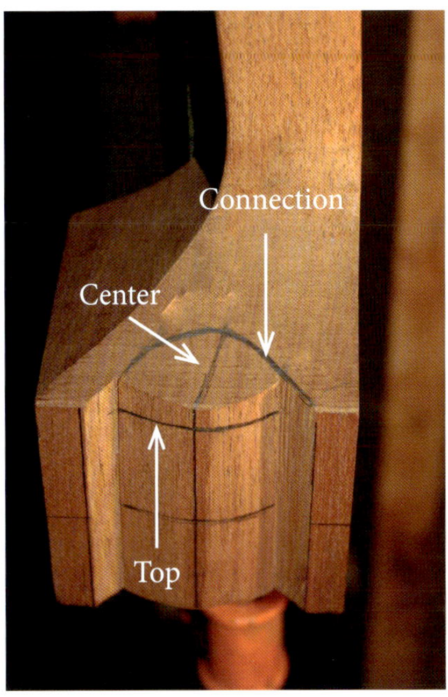

Figure 9-20. The section above the "top" bounded by "connection" will be removed. This will establish the top of the cylinder for the front section. Note that the "connection" line flows into the toe sides.

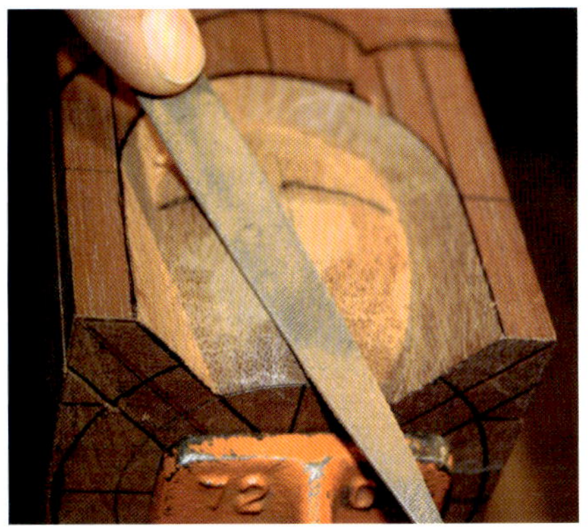

Figure 9-17. Use a small file to remove the remaining facets to form a smooth surface. The break point line should still be visible or mostly so.

Figure 9-19. Form a cylinder on one of the front sections. This is easier because the top of the ball is open.

Figure 9-21. Use a flat chisel to set in along the top line. To avoid undercutting the toe, use the toe side as a guide and reference.

The front faces are a little easier because the top is already exposed and the toe cuts are the required depth along the whole length. On a given front face, use a flat chisel to round over the section between the saw cuts to the outer circle. Most of the cuts can be made with the grain, but occasionally cross-grain cuts work better. Figure 9-19 shows the results.

Next sketch the curves shown in figure 9-20. The upper line labeled "top" is 2⅜" from the bottom and is the height of the ball in front. The line labeled "center" is the extension of the vertical centerline as it goes toward the ankle. Finally, the curve labeled "connection" connects the front and side toes and will be used to help establish the top of the ball. It does not have to be perfect because it is going to be completely removed later.

Starting in the center, use a flat chisel to set in along the top line as shown in figure 9-21. Be careful to keep the corner of the chisel from cutting into the side of the toe. Use the flat surface of the toe as a reference to guide the chisel. Now remove the material above the top line and bounded by the toe connecting curve. A #7 16 mm gouge fits the center part of the profile pretty well. The goal is to create a cylindrical section as a first step. Figure 9-22 shows early progress and figure 9-23 shows the operation complete.

In a manner similar to the back faces, round over the top and bottom portions of the cylindrical section. Recall that the "break point" line remains high and the surface falls off from there in both directions, top and bottom. The bottom section is identical to those on the back faces using the inner circle as the terminating curve. The top section rounds into the "U"-shaped surface connecting the toes. Theoretically, the highest point on this section of the ball is at the center of the "U" where it meets the top of the cylinder. The surface falls off from this point in all directions. As usual, I mostly use a ¾" flat chisel to rough-shape the sphere and a #3 25 mm gouge to refine it. Figures 9-24, 9-25, and 9-26 show increasing degrees of progress. Note how the toe heights increase as the sphere is formed from the cylinder. When the carving is complete, blend the facets with a flat file and clean up the file marks with sandpaper. Repeat these steps on the other front face.

Figures 9-27, 9-28, and 9-29 show what the foot should look like thus far. The ball has been extracted and the toes are isolated. At this point the Philadelphia foot and this Newport foot are the same, and the steps to get here are the same. The four spherical sections should more or less appear to be one surface with the toes sitting on top. From here forward there will be differences with the Philadelphia foot.

Figure 9-22. Use a #7 16 mm gouge to remove material above the top line.

Figure 9-23. Continue with the #7 up to the "connection" curve. The top of the cylinder is now set.

Figure 9-24. Start to convert the cylinder to a sphere. Remove the bottom corner down to the inner circle.

Figure 9-25. Keep the break point line high and blend toward the top and bottom.

Figure 9-26. Continue blending until a smooth, spherical surface results. Use a small file for final blending and cleanup.

Figure 9-27. The two spherical sections should appear as one surface with a toe on top.

Figure 9-28. The two back sections are complete and visually connected.

Figure 9-29. The ball as viewed from the front.

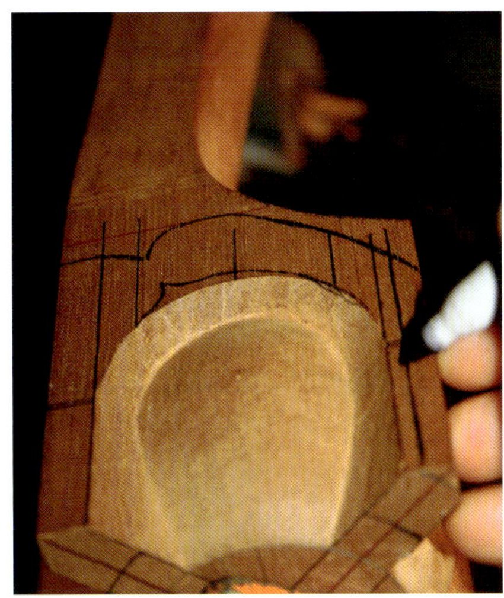

Figure 9-30. Draw guide lines for removing the top triangle of the side toe.

The next step is to define the side and back toes. Begin by establishing the height of the side toes. Start by removing the top corner so the toe stock is ½" proud of the ball. As shown in figure 9-30, make a mark ½" up from the inner circle on the bottom. Transfer this line up the sides of the toe as also shown in figure 9-30. Rasp the top corner down to this height. Figure 9-31 shows the result.

Now make marks 1⅜" and 1⅝" up from the bottom as shown in figure 9-32. The lower one is the height of the talon and the upper one is the high point of the lowest knuckle. From the upper mark, use a flat chisel to angle the surface following the profile of the toe on the side face as a guide. Carve in this way until there is a little more than ⅞" along the angled surface. Make a mark ⅞" up from the 1⅝" line on the angled surface as shown in figure 9-33. Using a flat chisel, blend from the ⅞" mark into the ankle. Figure 9-34 shows the result. The toe is now the proper height and transitions into the ankle nicely.

Next raise the side toe ankle bones and the back toe. Use a #11 5 mm gouge to carve along the top of the side and back toes as shown in figure 9-35. Bevel into these cuts as shown in figure 9-36. Repeat these steps until the side and back toes are ⅛" or a little more proud of the background. Figure 9-37 shows the desired outcome.

In a manner similar to the side toes, remove the corner on the back toe so that the remaining height is ½" proud of the ball.

Now separate the side toe from the back one. Sketch in the curves "A" and "B" shown in figure 9-38. These curves are a little tighter, blend into the lines of the toes, and touch at one point. Use a V-tool to separate the toes down to the ball as shown in figure 9-39. Blend the V-cut into the side surface of the back toe. Figure 9-40 shows the toes separated on one side and the ball side toe surfaces connected. Repeat these steps on the other side. Figure 9-41 shows the back toe fully isolated.

Figure 9-31. Use a rasp to remove the top section.

Figure 9-32. Mark the top of the cuticle 1⅜", and the center of the first knuckle 1⅝".

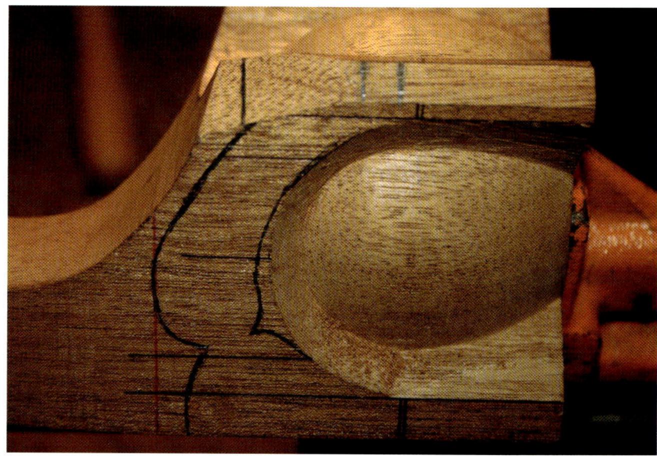

Figure 9-33. Mark the middle of the second knuckle ⅞" up from the first.

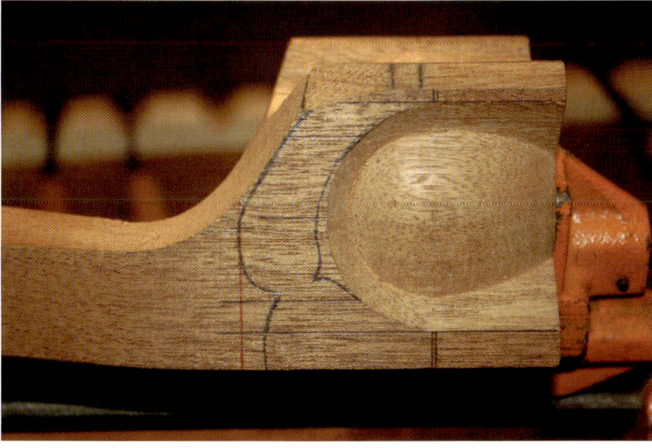

Figure 9-34. Remove the material above the second knuckle and blend the surface moving up the ankle.

Figure 9-35. Use a #11 5 mm gouge to separate the side and back toes.

Figure 9-36. Remove the material above the toe and blend the surface into the base of the toe cut.

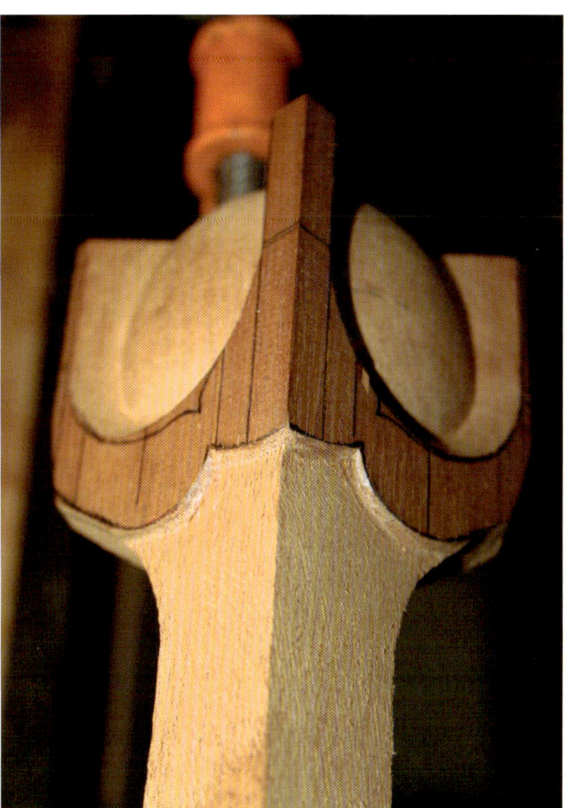

Figure 9-37. Both of the side toes and the back toe are separated and raised.

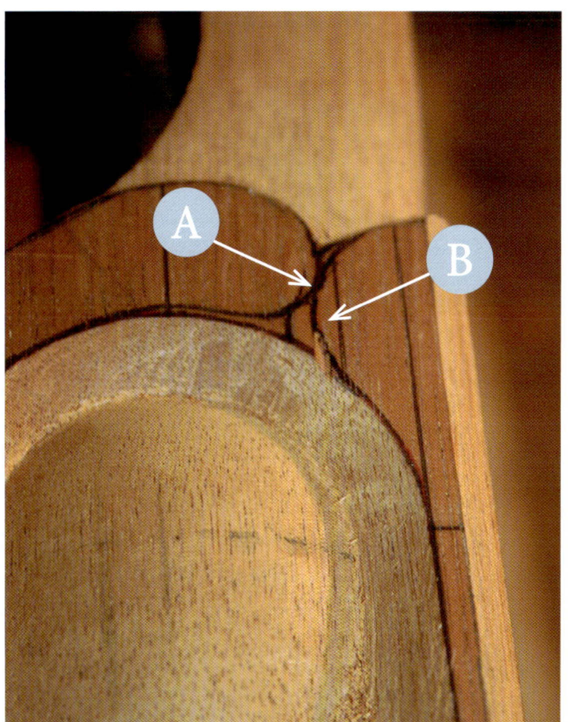

Figure 9-38. Draw the separation lines for the back and side toes. Blend each of the lines into their respective toe surfaces.

OPEN TALON BALL AND CLAW FOOT

The next step is to refine the back toe. Start by making marks on the back toe at 1⅜", 1⅝", and 2" from the bottom as shown in figure 9-42. Also make a mark at 1⅛" from the bottom on the side of the toe near the ball. This is also shown in figure 9-42. Connect this point to the center of the 1⅜" line. Sketch this line freehand using your eye as a guide. This angled line is the toe/claw boundary.

Use a #2 12 mm gouge to set in along this angled line. On the top of the toe, the bevel of the gouge will be away from the bottom, and on the sides the bevel will be toward the bottom. In each case be careful not to undercut the section of the toe above the claw. Angle the gouge acutely with the segment above the claw to accomplish this. Bevel into this stop cut from below, leaving about a 1/16" ridge. Figure 9-43 shows the result.

Use a rasp and/or file to round over the top portion of the upper toe segment as shown in figure 9-44. Redraw the line at 2" above the bottom. Use a #9 10 mm gouge to cut a trough at the 2" line. Cut across the top and down both sides. Figure 9-45 shows the idea.

The next step is to round the portion above the trough cut into a bulbous surface and blend it smoothly into the narrow section just above the claw. This is a bit tedious and less deterministic, because very small amounts of wood are removed at a time in many iterations and the shape is determined by eye. Use a #3 gouge or a flat chisel to shape the bulb. There is no exact way to do this, so use whatever chisel works, and keep in mind the goal—a bulbous, smooth surface. Start by removing the corners and refine from there. Figure 9-46 shows intermediate progress and figure 9-47 shows the operation complete. Clean up the final facets with a small file, a scraper, and sandpaper.

Next work on the back claw. All of the claws are the same size and they are done exactly the same way. Draw the lines labeled "A" and "B" in figure 9-48. "A" is ⅛" above the circle on the bottom of the foot. "B" defines the envelope for the claw. Note that the bottom of the curve is at the ⅛" line. Also note that the claw curve touches the toe a little below the top. This sets the claw a little below the toe, which is the desired effect. Use a flat chisel to remove the material above the curved line just drawn. Figure 9-49 shows this step.

Figure 9-39. Use a V-tool to cut around each toe line. Blend the cuts into the surface as shown.

Figure 9-40. Further blend the V-cut into the side toe surface above the ball.

Figure 9-41. Repeat the process on the other side so the back toe is completely separated.

Figure 9-43. Separate the claw from the toe along the angled boundary line.

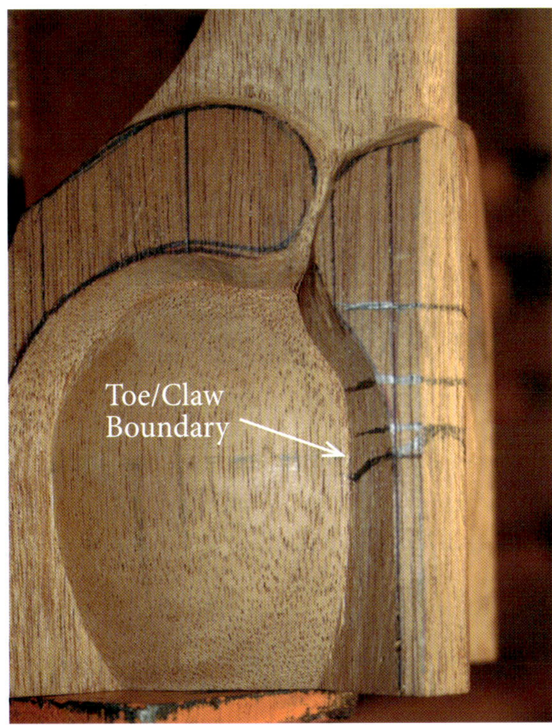

Figure 9-42. Mark the various detail heights using the numbers in figure 9-3. The "toe/claw boundary" is an angled line.

Figure 9-44. Round the toe surface above the claw to a cylindrical section.

OPEN TALON
BALL AND CLAW FOOT

The claw narrows as it goes to the bottom, so draw lines as shown in figure 9-50. The width of the claw at the bottom is ⅛". Make marks 1⁄16" on either side of the centerline. With your eye as a guide, connect each of the 1⁄16" marks with the full thickness of the claw at the top. Use a flat chisel to remove the waste on the outside of the line as shown in figure 9-51. Take a series of thin cuts from the top surface of the claw toward the ball. Be mindful of the grain and come at if from a different angle if necessary. Be careful not to mar the surface of the ball with the downward cuts. The surfaces underneath these outer sections are a continuation of the ball, so they are slightly curved. Use a #3 20 mm gouge to carry the curvature of the ball into the tapered claw side. Figure 9-52 shows both sides tapered with the surface of the ball extended.

Now the tapered wedge needs to be rounded. Rounding the top surface is done as a series of bevel approximations. Freehand a centerline as shown in figure 9-52. Use a flat chisel to remove the initial corners and then bevel the newly formed facets to approximate a curve. After a couple of iterations with the chisel, use a small file and sandpaper to blend the facets. Strive for a smooth and uniform surface. Figure 9-53 shows early progress and figure 9-54 shows the completed surface.

The last step on this toe, for now, is to refine the cuticle on the sides. The idea is to remove the corner as shown in figure 9-54. Use a #7 6 mm gouge for this. Position the gouge so that the arc of the gouge blends nicely with the top portion and cuts off the corner at the ball. Figure 9-55 shows the cut complete. Finally, round the square shoulder just created down to the surface of the claw. The back toe and claw are done for now. The claw will be undercut later.

Figure 9-45. The back toe has a bulbous top portion. Use a #9 10 mm gouge to cut along the 2" height line. Continue this cut down to the ball on both sides.

Figure 9-46. Round the edges of the gouge cut to from a bulb on the upper portion and narrower section below.

Figure 9-47. Refine the surface until it is smooth and uniform and the curves look good.

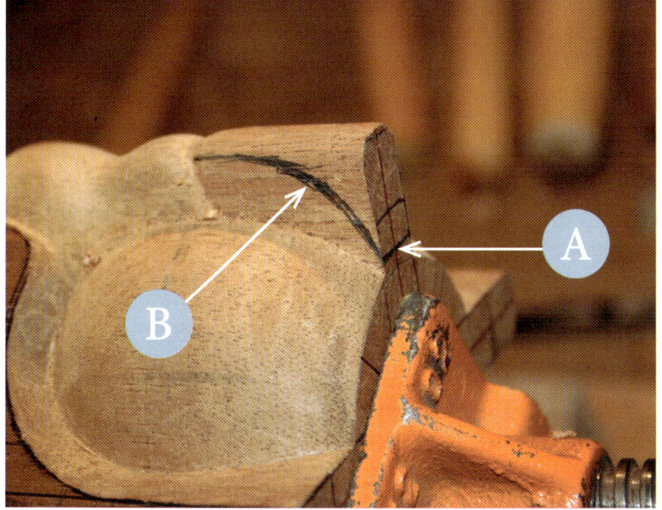

Figure 9-48. Establish the claw. The perimeter of the claw is an arc that goes from line "A" to the base of the cut at the toe/claw boundary. The claw height is a little below the toe height.

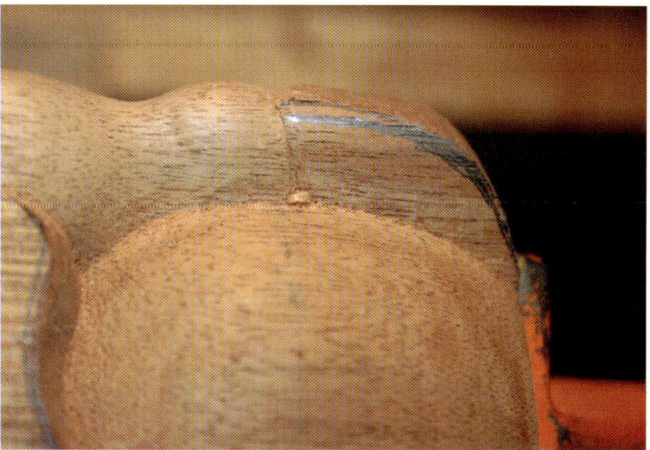

Figure 9-49. Remove the material above the claw arc with a flat chisel.

Figure 9-50. The claw narrows side-to-side as it approaches the bottom. Draw the symmetric guide lines to determine the taper.

Next work on one of the front faces to separate the toes. Start by drawing the lines shown in figure 9-56. The lines labeled "A" are ⅛" from their respective edges and are needed to define the tendons that run from the toes into the ankle. The line labeled "B" is about 1⅜" from the bottom and at the height of the side toe knuckle. The vertex of the lines labeled "C" is the midpoint of the width of the ankle between the tendon lines. Also add the tendon line on the back face as shown in figure 9-57. This is ⅛" from the front face.

Use a larger V-tool to remove the material between the lines "C" as shown in figure 9-57.

Figure 9-58 shows early progress and figure 9-59 shows the step complete. The surface at the bottom of the V-cut is the ball, so blend it to what is already there.

Next isolate the tendons. Use a #11 5 mm gouge to make the cuts shown in figure 9-60. With a ½" flat chisel, round over the edges of the center section as shown in figure 9-61. Deepen the tendon cuts and repeat the rounding until the tendon is about ⅛" deep. The depth adds visual tension to the tendons, which there is a lot of in this leg. Figure 9-62 shows later progress.

Now work on the back side of the same tendon. Use a #11 5 mm gouge to make the cuts shown in figure 9-63. On the cut that follows the side toe on its top, run the gouge cut out the front face. Position the tendon so that it flows somewhere near the middle of the toe segment. Blend the background into the bottom of these cuts as shown in figure 9-64.

Because this rounded section between the tendons blends into the toes, the toes need to be rounded to complete the transition. Set the toe segment heights as shown in figure 9-65. The claw and first knuckle heights are the same for all the toes. On the side toes, the middle of the second knuckle is ⅞" from the middle of the first one. Use a flat chisel to blend whatever is above the second knuckle into the next segment up the ankle. Round over the individual segments to form a tube. Figure 9-66 shows progress.

Round over the bulbous part of the side toe and blend it into the segment on the front face. Figure 9-67 shows the idea. Use the same techniques as before to shape and detail the claw for this toe. Figure 9-68 shows the claw shaped and the cuticle above it formed.

Use a #9 10 mm gouge to make the cuts between the knuckle segments as shown in figure 9-69. These cuts are across the top and down to the ball on each side. Round over the edges to form separate tubular segments as shown in figure 9-70. This is a standard technique on all ball and claw feet.

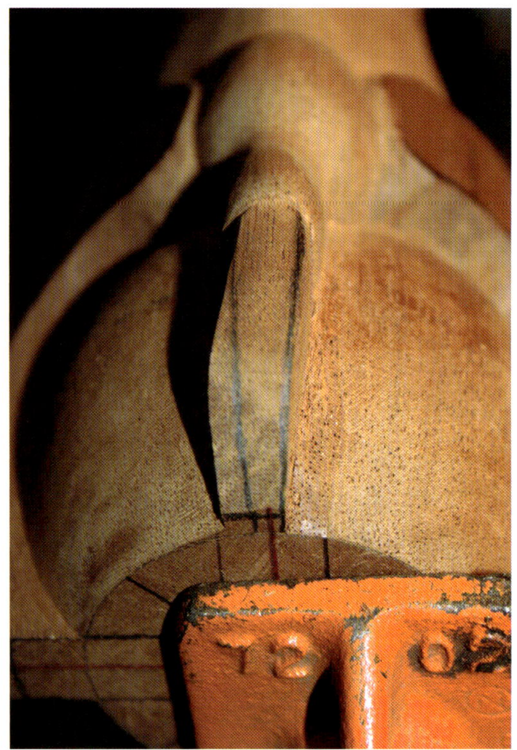

Figure 9-51. Use a ¾" flat chisel to taper the claw. Do this in several small cuts. The grain may be an issue here, so be careful not to let it tear out.

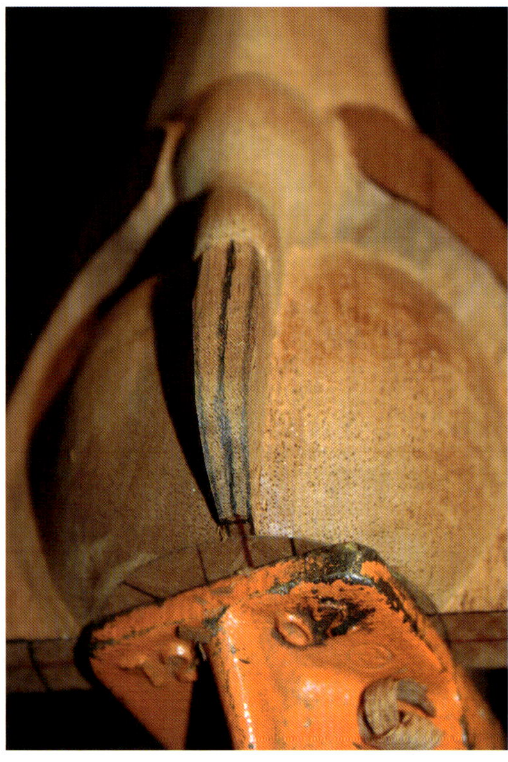

Figure 9-52. Form the taper on the other side. Note that the surface beneath the removed material is the ball, so it must blend into the surrounding area.

Figure 9-53. Round the top of the claw into a nice, curved surface and blend it into the walls on the side.

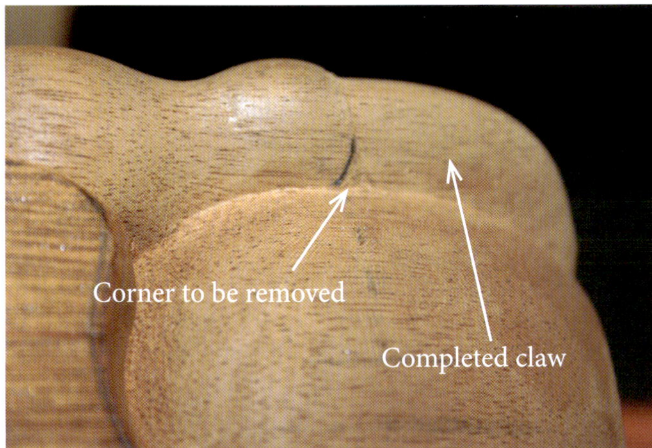

Figure 9-54. The cuticle just above the claw has a rounded tip. Use a #7 6 mm gouge to cut a curve that blends well. Round the edges of the cut slightly to soften the line. Let your eye be the guide as to what looks good.

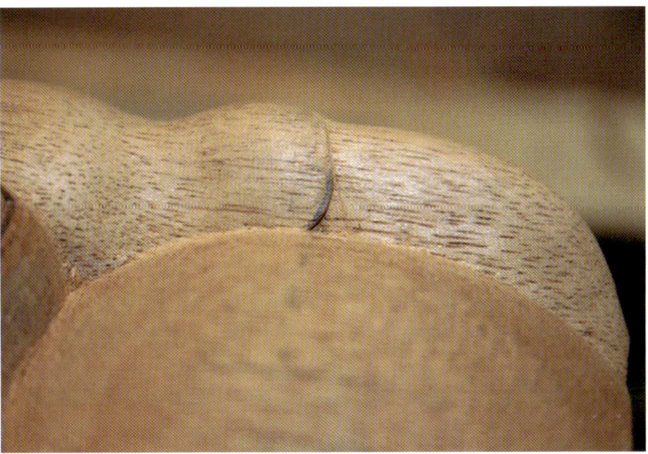

Figure 9-55. The cuticle is finished and the toe and claw are complete for now. The toe will be undercut later.

Figure 9-56. Determine the front side landmarks. These guides help position the elements so they will fit together. They also connect existing surfaces. The lines "B" are extensions of the toes as they meet on the top of the foot.

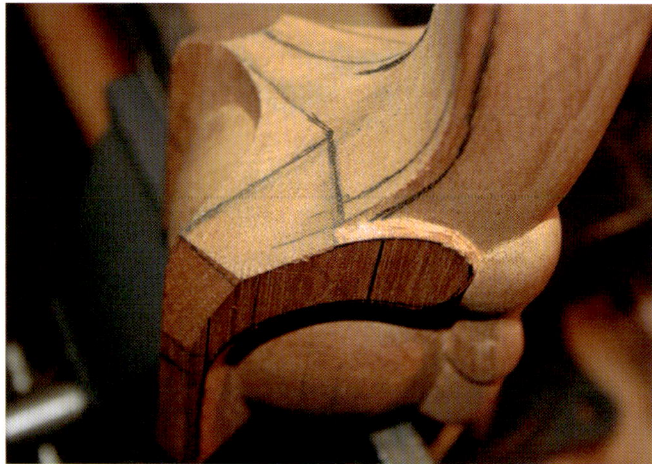

Figure 9-57. The tendon line in the side is ⅛" from the front face.

Figure 9-60. Separate the tendons on the front face. The tendons are narrow transition elements that connect the toes to the ankle. They add visual tension to the claws that hold the ball.

Figure 9-58. Use a larger V-tool to separate the toes. Be careful not to damage the ball surface.

Figure 9-61. Round the surface of the ankle between the tendons. The high spot is in the middle and it flows into the vertex of the toes.

Figure 9-59. Blend the surfaces into the toe sides.

Figure 9-62. Deepen the tendon cuts to ⅛". With each iteration blend the surrounding surfaces again.

Figure 9-63. Separate the tendon on the back face and deepen the side toe with a #11 5 mm gouge.

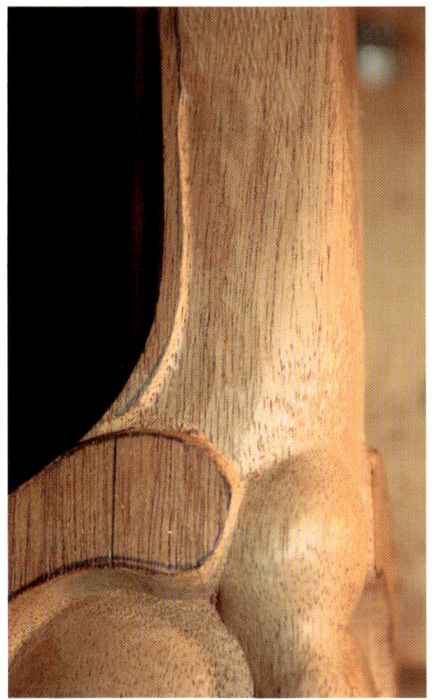

Figure 9-64. Blend the background into the base of the tendon and toe cuts.

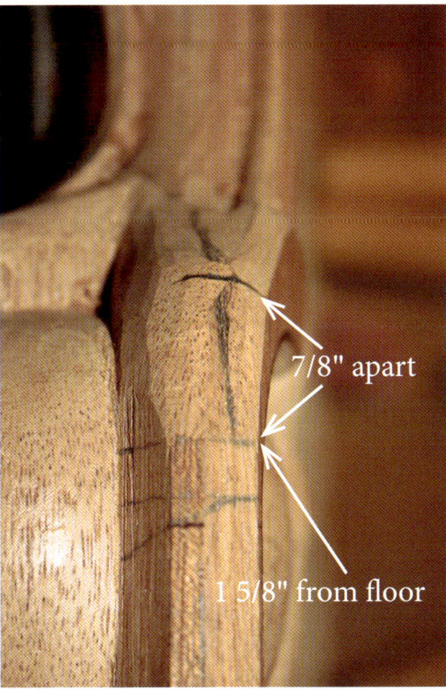

Figure 9-65. Establish the knuckle heights as shown. Use the numbers in figure 9-2.

Figure 9-66. Round each segment to form a cylindrical tube.

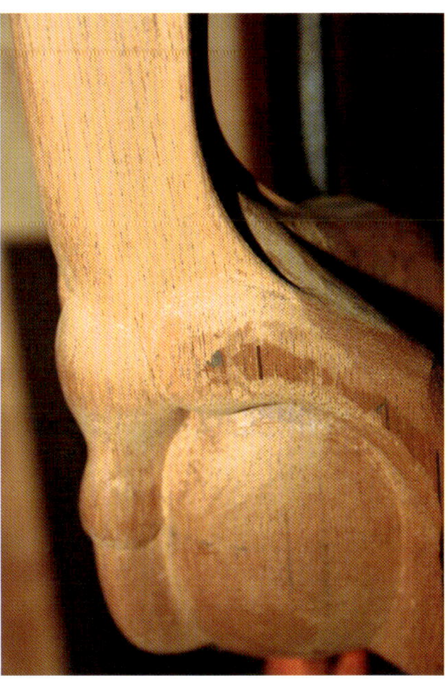

Figure 9-67. The bulbous portion of the side toe blends into the tube of the toe.

Figure 9-68. Shape the toe and claw as before.

OPEN TALON BALL AND CLAW FOOT

This toe is a little thick, so it needs to be thinned a bit. The lines in figure 9-71 show how much to thin it. This is not a lot, but it will make a big visual difference. Carve to the lines on each side with a flat chisel or a #2 gouge. Round over the corners and blend into the surrounding surface. Figure 9-72 shows the thinned toe. This toe is now complete.

Next work on the front toe. First repeat the layout for the other side toe and cut the "V" as shown in figure 9-73. Establish the tendons and round the field between them as before. Figure 9-74 shows progress. Establish and shape the claw on the front toe using the same techniques as before. Draw the toe segments as shown in figure 9-75. The middle of the first knuckle is 1⅝" from the bottom and the second is ⅞" from the first. The front toe has a third segment, which is ¾" from the second. Form the tubular segments as before, blending any extra length from a lower segment into the one above it using a flat chisel.

After each of the segments has been defined, use a #9 10 mm gouge to scoop the top and sides of each segment as shown in figure 9-76. Round all of the edges and facets as before, blending them into a smooth, flowing surface. Figure 9-77 shows the result.

Figure 9-69. Separate the toe tube into segments. The knuckle centerlines remain high and the area between two knuckles is lower. Use a #9 10 mm gouge to cut a trough between adjacent knuckles. Round the edges.

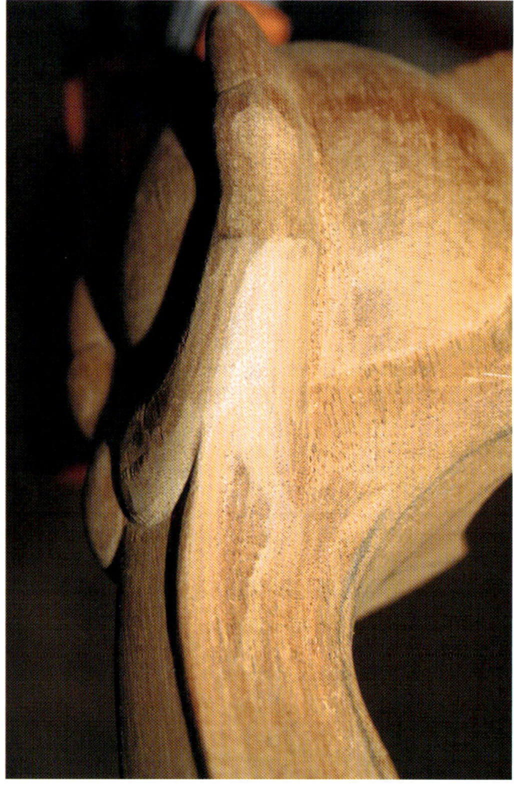

Figure 9-70. The toe segments after shaping.

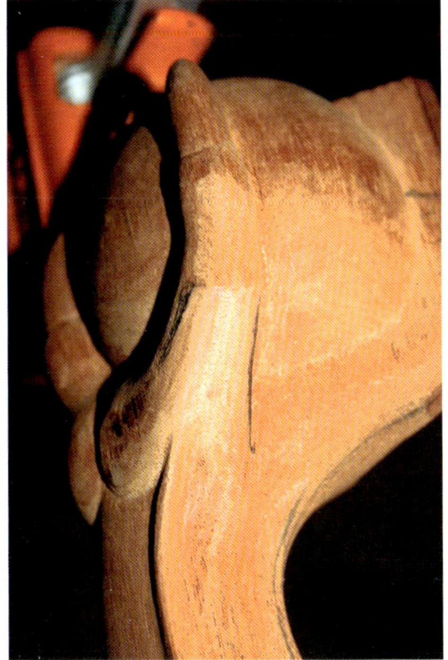

Figure 9-71. The upper segment is a little thick, so thin it out a bit. The lines determine what needs to be removed.

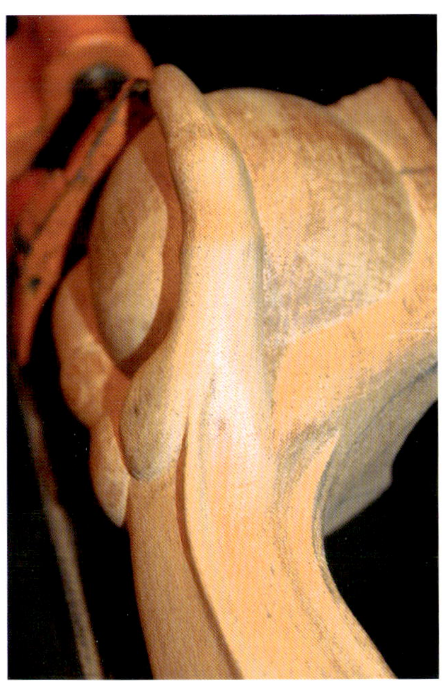

Figure 9-72. Use a flat chisel to cut to the thinning lines. Round and blend the surfaces.

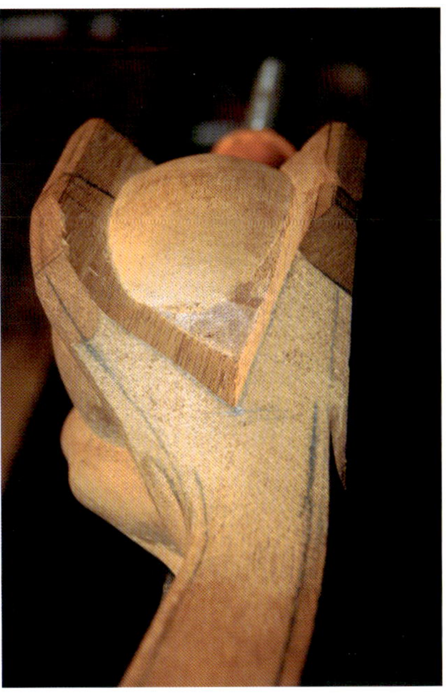

Figure 9-73. Complete the other side toe. This needs to be done before you can work on the front toe.

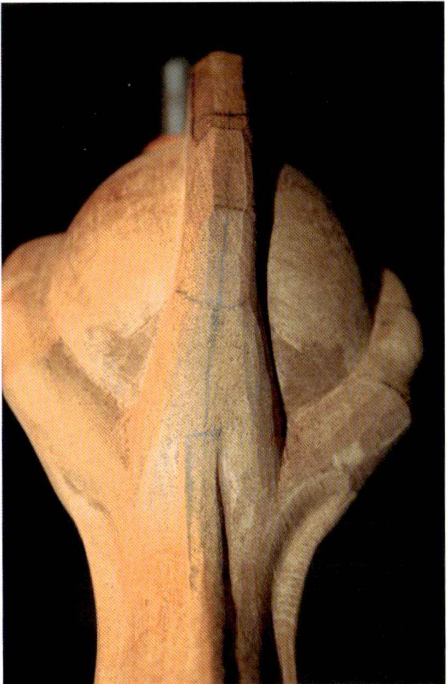

Figure 9-74. The front toe is ready to be shaped.

Figure 9-75. Use the numbers from figure 9-2 to mark the segments on the front toe.

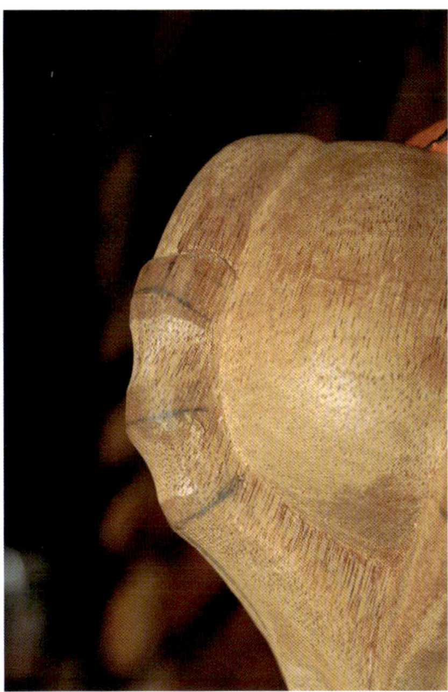

Figure 9-76. Shape the individual toe segments as before.

OPEN TALON BALL AND CLAW FOOT

Complete the remaining side toe. At this point the foot is complete, except for the undercutting. Figures 9-78 and 9-79 show the foot from different angles.

The next step is to open a space in each of the talons. This is one of the defining characteristics of this foot. Use your finger as a guide to draw the line shown in figure 9-80. Point "A" is ¼" up from the bottom and point "B" is ¼" above the ball. The strategy is to remove half the material from each side and meet in the middle. Use a #5 8 mm gouge to set in along the line as shown in figure 9-81. The angle between the chisel and the toe behind it is less than 90°. I do this so I don't put too much pressure on the claw. As material is removed, clean out the underside of the claw so that the cut is 90° to the side. Use a #1 1 mm chisel to cut the waste around the cuticle as shown in figure 9-82. This is an iterative process, so just remove a little material at a time. Figures 9-83 and 9-84 show early and intermediate progress. Figure 9-85 shows some early cleanout using the #1 1 mm chisel.

Figure 9-77. The front toe is complete.

Figure 9-78. All of the toes are complete. This image shows a side view.

Figure 9-79. A view from the back. Note how the ball is visually continuous across the toe.

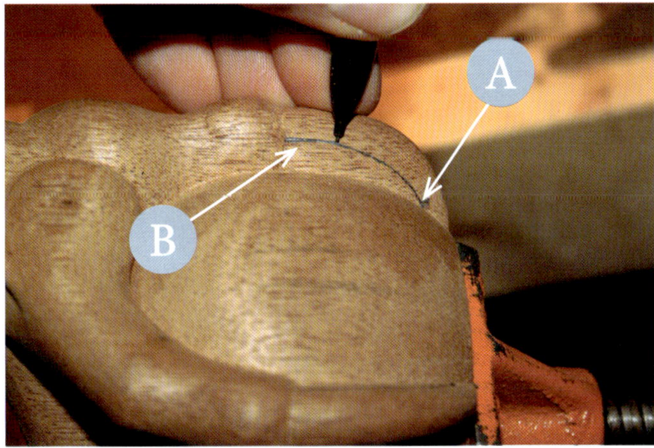

Figure 9-80. Draw the arc that defines the open portion of the claw. Point "A" is ¼" up from the bottom and point "B" is ¼" up from the surface of the ball. Draw this arc freehand to follow the line of the claw and hit the points "A" and "B."

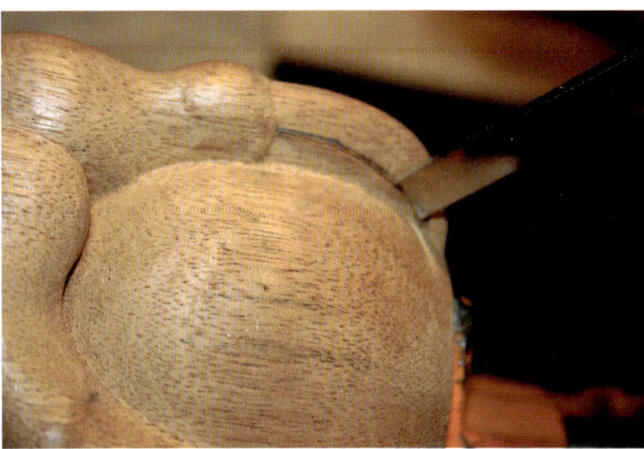

Figure 9-83. When some of the initial material is gone, repeat the steps to deepen the cut along the arc.

Figure 9-81. Start from a little below the arc and cut down toward the ball.

Figure 9-84. Deepen the cut to about halfway under the claw.

Figure 9-82. Cut around the curve of the cuticle with a small, flat chisel.

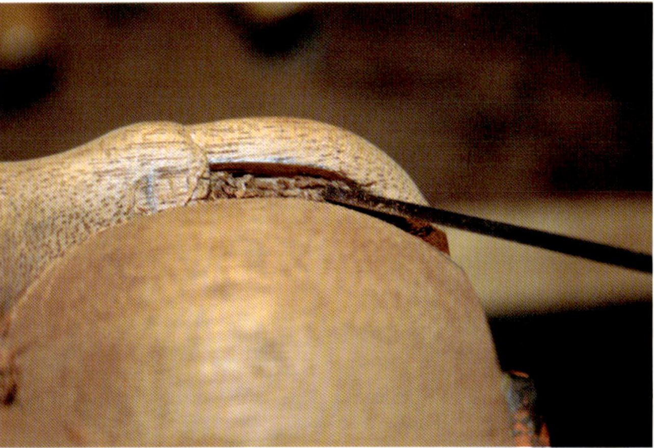

Figure 9-85. Use a narrow, relatively flat chisel to remove material under the middle of the claw. As the hole gets bigger and access improves, work to get the ceiling of the hole parallel to the ball.

Switch to the other side and repeat these steps. Figure 9-86 shows more progress and a small hole. Remove the remaining material and clean up the surface using a small file as shown in figure 9-87 for the final step. Remember that the surface at the bottom of the opening is the ball. So put a slight curvature to the surface when connecting one side to the other.

Figure 9-88 shows the opening almost complete. Use a small skew chisel to get into the tight space at the bottom of the foot. Figure 9-89 shows the claw opening complete. Repeat these steps to open the other claws.

What remains now is to open the top of the ball underneath the toes. This is a tedious and highly iterative process that is done by working from all angles to meet in the middle. Start by shaving a little material off the top of the ball as shown in figure 9-90. Then take some off the bottom of the toes just above shaved ball top as shown in figure 9-91. Repeat this a few times until the toe is noticeably undercut. Then move to the back of the same toe. I like to work on the side toes first because the distance to the back is shorter. Once a breakthrough is made, it is easier to see where material needs to be removed and there is better access.

When taking material off the top of the ball, remember that it descends to meet the back portions in a smooth and continuous surface, so angle the chisel accordingly. I use a 3 mm and a 12 mm skew chisel as well as a #1 1 mm straight chisel a lot in this process because the spaces are so tight. Also use slicing motions when possible and take a little material at a time so that less pressure is needed. As the bottom of the toes become available because of undercutting, round the corners to blend into the upper portions. This is needed visually and it will open the space a little more so there is easier access to or for? the next iteration.

Figure 9-92 shows progress after several iterations on both sides of the side toe. Note the small breakthrough. As a breakthrough is made, angle the toe side cuts up to form a dome-like surface on top of the ball. This helps the access and gives a visual sense of lift.

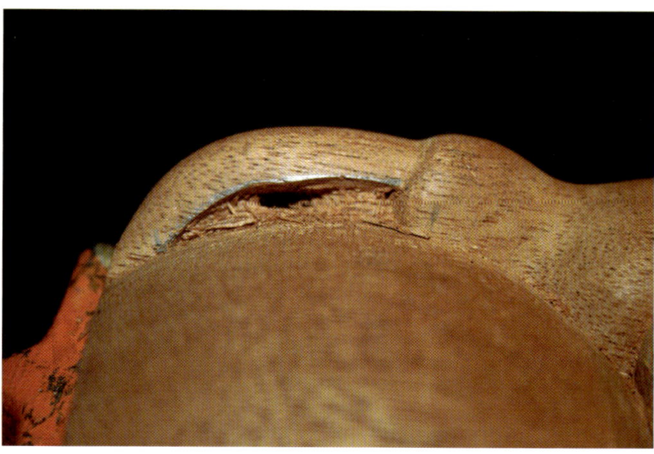

Figure 9-86. After progress is about halfway on one side, repeat the steps on the other. Soon a breakthrough hole will appear.

Figure 9-87. Increase the size of the hole to conform to the arc of the opening and the surface of the ball. Take shallow shavings so as not to put too much pressure on the claw. Clean up the surface of the ball with a small, flat file. There should be a slight curvature here because it is the extension of the sphere that is the ball.

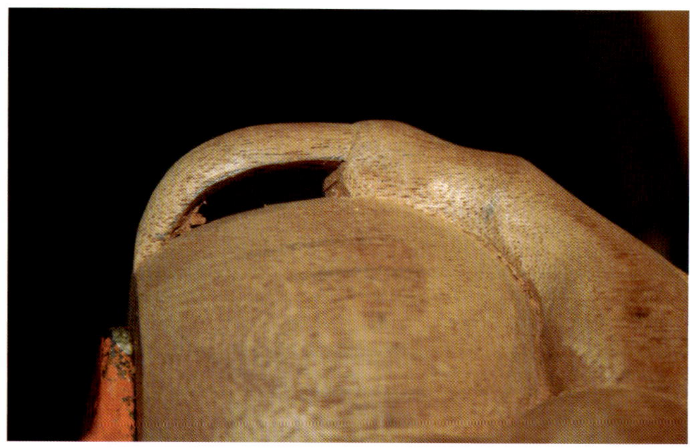

Figure 9-88. The area under the claw near the foot is especially tight. Avoid prying in here or the claw will break. Use a small skew chisel with a slicing motion to get into this tight area.

Figure 9-89. The opening is complete. Repeat this process on the other three claws.

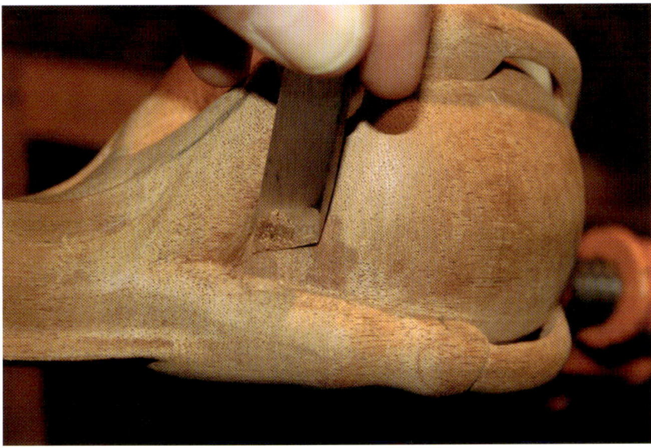

Figure 9-90. Use the leading point of a skew chisel to remove some of the ball underneath the toes.

Figure 9-91. Remove some material from the bottom of the toes. Repeat this and the last operation several times, going deeper under the toes each time. After several iterations on one side of the toe, do the same steps on the other side of the same toe.

Figure 9-92. Alternate between both sides of a single toe until a small breakthrough is made.

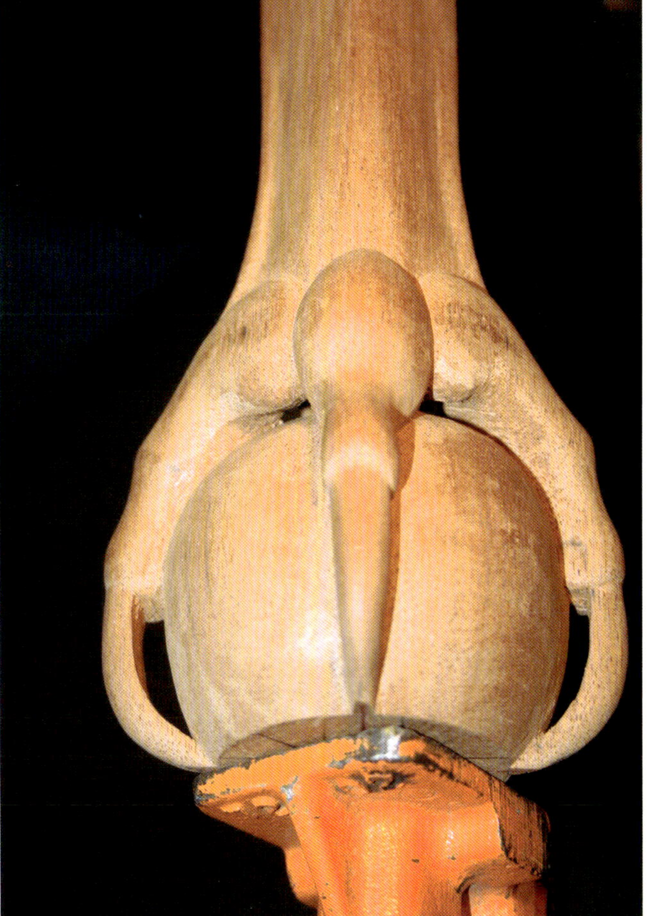

Figure 9-93. Progress after many iterations on multiple toes.

OPEN TALON BALL AND CLAW FOOT

After a breakthrough on one of the side toes, work on the other side. Figure 9-93 shows the two side toe openings. Then work to connect each side with the middle, working from both sides of the center toe. Figure 9-94 shows an opening underneath the center toe. Use a small, flat file to blend the facets on top of the ball underneath the toes to a smooth surface.

The foot is now complete. Figures 9-95, 9-96, and 9-97 show the completed foot from various angles. In figure 9-97, note the depth of the tendons and how the areas between them transition from the toes to the ankle. They blend into the leg background about 6" up from the bottom.

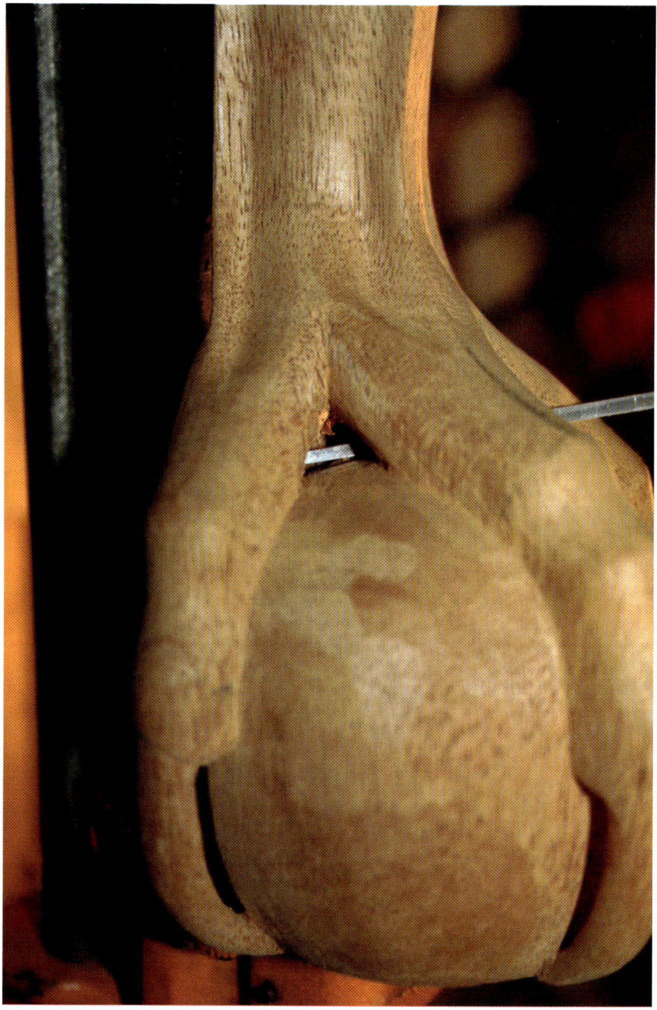

Figure 9-94. This opening is about right.

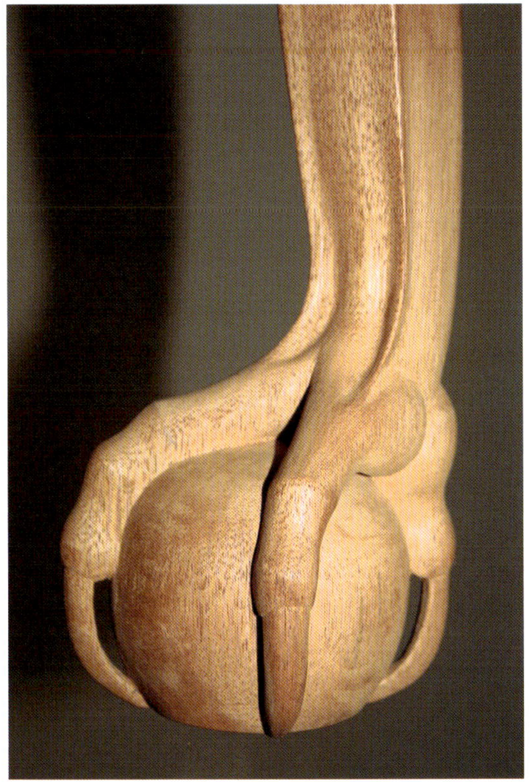
Figure 9-95.

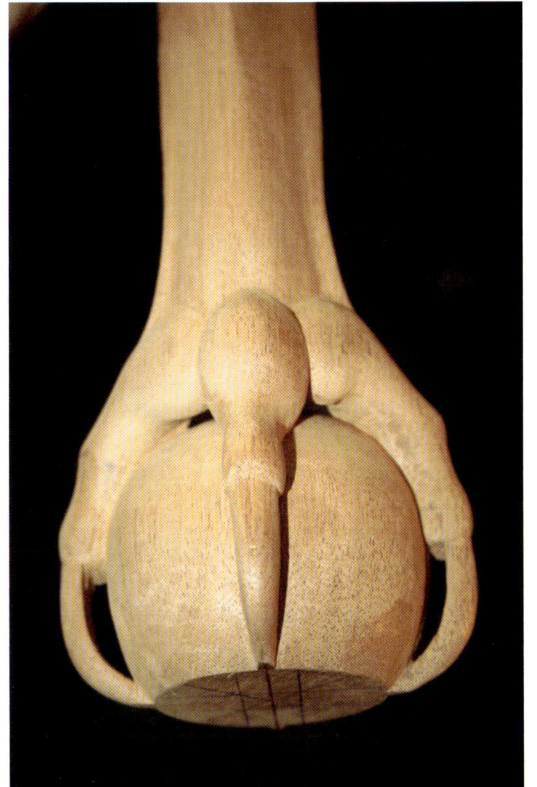
Figure 9-96.

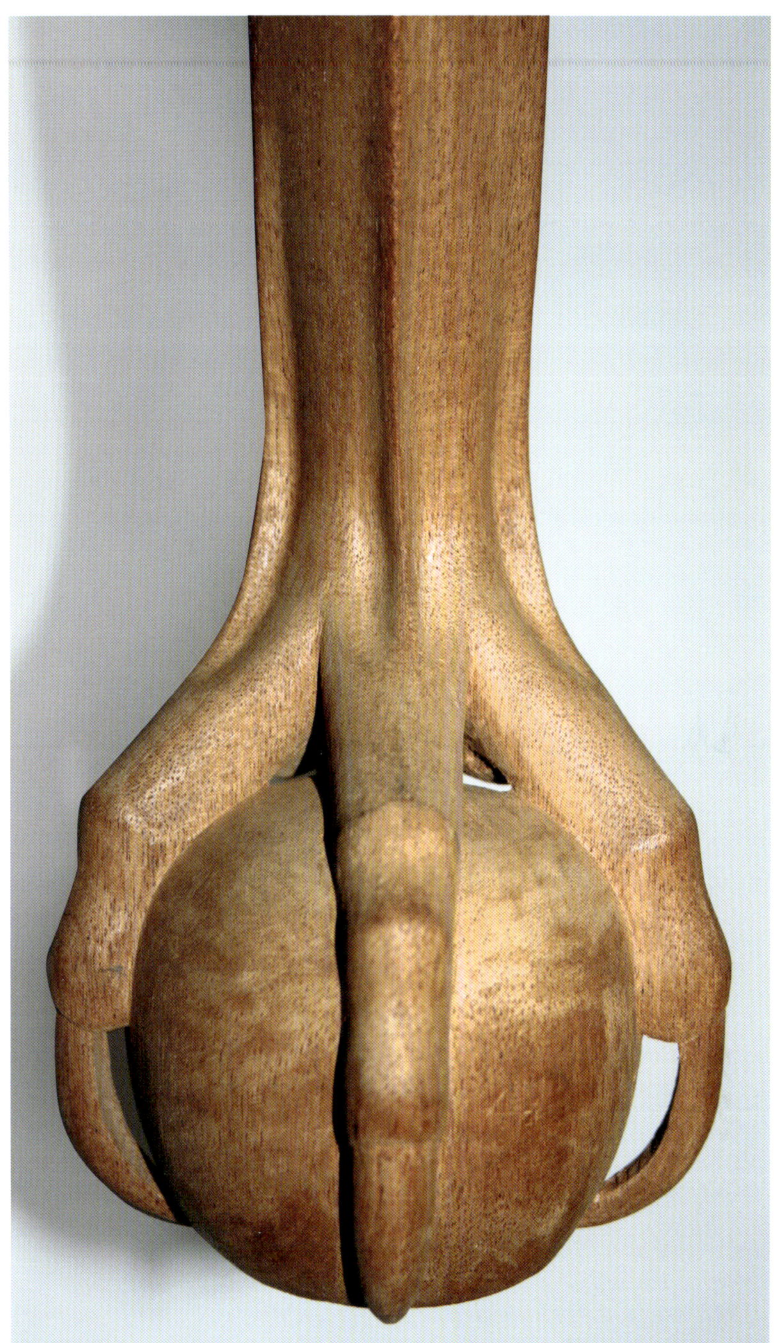
Figure 9-97.

Tony Kubalak builds Queen Anne and Chippendale reproductions in his basement workshop in Eagan, Minnesota. He specializes in faithfully reproducing the finest pieces of eighteenth-century American furniture. Tony studied with Gene Landon at the Olde Mill Cabinet Shoppe, and his work has been featured in *Fine Woodworking*, *Woodwork*, *Woodshop News*, *Eagan* magazine, and *Midwest Home*. He is the author of *Carving 18th Century American Furniture Elements* and has written articles for national magazines including *American Period Furniture*, the annual journal of the Society of American Period Furniture Makers. Tony's work has won awards for Best Carving, Best Handwork, and Best Traditional Design at the Northern Woods Exhibition, an annual display and competition sponsored by the Minnesota Woodworkers Guild. He has been recognized nationally for nine consecutive years by being selected for the Directory of Traditional American Crafts, sponsored by *Early American Life* magazine. See more of his work at www.tonykubalak.com.